# Wake

# HER

# UP

*By* Marcella Hill

Edited by Lil Barcaski and Linda Hinkle

Published by: GWN Publishing

www.GWNPublishing.com

Cover Design: Kristina Conatser Captured by KC Designs

ISBN: 979-8-9867817-0-9

## This Book is Dedicated to

*The women that lived without ever waking up.*
*This book and my awakening are dedicated to you.*

# CONTENTS

# (INTRODUCTION TO MYSELF)

At 30 years old, I sat crying on the floor of my parent's basement; this was now my bedroom and my home. No little voices calling for Mommy. No snacks to clean up. No sippy cups to fill. No one coming home at 5 o'clock for dinner. No one to ask, "How was work?"

No bedtime stories. No goodnight kisses. Bedtime was now me, alone, brushing my teeth in silence. I didn't recognize this life. Without being a mother and a wife, I had no idea who I was. I had woken up to a world where I didn't exist.

In becoming a wife, I thought I had found my identity. I was a **WIFE**. And when children came, I was a **MOTHER**. Each title, a puzzle piece that would eventually create a whole picture of *me*. People with the most titles seemed more complete. The woman that could say, "I'm a doctor, a mother, a wife, a home-owner, a size 8, a board member, an artist, a baker, a volunteer," was the whole picture of a successful human. The more titles, the more the person.

There I was, in my parent's basement with one title, Ex-wife a negative title. I would have to make up for it. Eventually, the tears would run out, and the journey of finding and collecting myself would start all over again.

*Isn't this what everyone is doing? Isn't this the entire point of life? To find yourself?* I was taught to marry a man of my same faith, to start a family, and that being a mother would bring me the most fulfillment and happiness. Being a *Mother* was who I was meant to be. If I checked all the right boxes, I thought I was promised a happy life.

A successful day ends with all the boxes checked. The longer the list, the more productive the day. The more productive the day, the more successful the human. A list of unchecked boxes equaled a day of failure. Sometimes I would add mundane things to the list, just to be able to earn the check marks. Brush teeth **CHECK**. Eat lunch **CHECK**. If daily checkmarks meant a successful day, then life checkmarks meant a successful existence.

When my marriage ended after nine years, all that work went up in flames. My checked boxes were torn up and thrown away, as if they never mattered at all. Without being a wife, I was half of me. No more title of **WIFE**. When I moved out and left my children for the summer, the other half was gone. I had no idea that I could be somebody without the titles that defined me.

After months of tears and anger, I jumped into collecting my pieces. I quickly remarried - wife, **CHECK**! I had my kids during the school year, plus we had a baby of our own... Mother, **CHECK**! I even got an amazing job... Employee, **CHECK**! I was back! And even better, I had added a few titles.

This was it, here I am! I had found myself again. Life was good. My check marks were checked.

When I was fired from my dream job, I felt again that I had lost a piece of myself. After more tears and more anger, I acquired my parent's business. I found a great passion for the brand and thought, *Here I am! Successful business owner, Mother, Wife. I've found myself... again!*

This...**THIS** was **ME**! Life was good. I just have to keep all the boxes checked.

My oldest daughter became a teenager. Things got difficult. She moved out to live with her Dad. Once again, another piece of me was gone; I had failed to keep one of the essential pieces. The big piece. The *mother* piece. This was a piece I couldn't replace.

There I was, crying in a dark place, wondering who I was without being her mother. Being a mother was making her breakfast and doing her laundry. No after school chats. No telling her to clean her room or turn the lights off for bed. *How do I be her mother without all the mothering things?* If I couldn't be her mother, I would never be complete.

*If I couldn't be complete, then what was the point?* I had failed. No amount of collecting pieces would fill this gap. Being in this familiar darkness was the moment I knew I had to wake up. The suffocating darkness was going to swallow me up and never let me go. It was a nightmare I had had over and over.

I was exhausted and so freaking sick of falling apart every time someone didn't want me. There had to be something else. There had to be a way to wake up from this endless loop of dead ends. *Was there a way to go to bed every night as a whole person, no matter what happened? Could I be someone without the checklist? Could I be someone without the titles?*

During this same time period, a friend recommended the book, *A Man's Search for Meaning*, by Victor Frankl. This man tells his story of finding purpose while in a concentration camp. He had all of his titles taken. His entire family was gone, his clothes, his hair, his home ... everything that would define a human's existence. And yet, he found he had purpose and identity. This sparked a light to a new day, questions I hadn't thought to ask, a light I hadn't noticed before.

If he could find himself in the midst of the most devastating environment in world history, surely, I could find myself when people didn't like me. I could be a whole person when I lose a job. I could exist, all of me, when anything bad happened. I was awake to the idea that I am not my titles, or my things. Who was this girl that I had lived with my whole life and somehow had never met?

I started asking myself every morning, *Who is Marcella?* I sat quietly and listened to what was in me. *What was bugging me? What were my thoughts? What did She need?* Then I would try and do that. I called it, *Being Me On Purpose.* There was no checklist. No reporting. No workbook to finish or classes to attend. Just me asking who I was every day. I tried it for 100 days. I fizzled out around day 50 and then came back around on day 75.

And guess what!? I found myself! Paying attention was sometimes as simple as, *Does Marcella need to watch Netflix or listen to a podcast?* And I ended up listening to uplifting podcasts. *What is bugging me today?* The laundry has bugged me all week. I would do the laundry that day. *Where can I be useful?* I would meet up with a friend. New ideas came. I read books that brought clarity and understanding. I wrote. I even went to an adult dance class. I started seeing myself. I started hearing myself. I started noticing how things were different when I showed up. I noticed feelings, fears that I hadn't seen before, and distractions I hadn't been willing to acknowledge, past trauma that was still in my way. I woke up to all of me.

I met **HER**. The girl inside. *Why haven't I ever talked to Her before!?* I found a soul inside me. She has taught me that I am not my titles, I am not my body, and I'm not even my thoughts. I am a whole being, and when things and people come and go, she remains a whole being.

No more collecting pieces. No more losing them and starting over. I had been a whole *me* the entire time. Knowing that I wasn't scattered pieces waiting to be found changed everything, even my everyday interactions.

My husband could say something crappy to me, and I was okay. Maybe he was having a bad day. My daughter could say things that used to break me apart, and now I could stay whole and even be useful. The car could break down, plans could be changed, bad things could happen, and there I was, still all of me.

Getting to know myself is a journey that will last my entire life. Learning to let myself live beyond my human fears and ideas may take an eternity. But those moments when I have allowed Her to wake up and live have resulted in miracles beyond my imagination. They have kept me whole and even useful during situations that used to leave me in a dark place, questioning who I am. Knowing Her has mended relationships and provided peace in the middle of chaos. Knowing that I am not here to piece myself together, but to get to know the woman I already am, has allowed me freedom and joy that I didn't know existed.

When I know that I am whole, I don't need someone to love me. I don't need my bank account to tell me who I am. I don't need my titles. I'm not waiting for someone or something to tell me who I am. I am not collecting myself in every experience. I am here to add to the world.

### *The world is no longer happening to me. I was made to happen to the world.*

I felt like something was missing for so long. If only I could find just the right thing, I would finally be whole. That thing that I was missing was Me, like missing someone you love so dearly. A longing for something you can't explain. A missing of someone you have yet to meet. It is **YOU**. The woman inside.

Do you feel it? The spark, the stirring, the knocking? She's been there the whole time. It is time to wake her up, get to know Her, and let Her live. How do you know she's there? A beautiful book by Michael Singer, *The Untethered Soul*, was one of the first examples that explicitly explains how we exist behind our thoughts. I read his words and did what he suggested and **THERE SHE WAS**. It went something like this—Try screaming in your mind. Do it, actually scream inside, right now. Did you hear that? There **YOU** are. Not the girl screaming, the one listening to it. **YOU** are the girl inside.

Imagine waking up every day, no matter what is happening in your life or the world and **KNOWING** you will go to bed a **WHOLE** being. No one and nothing can take away pieces. You don't have to keep searching for yourself. You are not lost. You are not broken. You, the girl inside, knows exactly who She is, why She was created, and She's waiting for you to get to know Her enough to help Her do what She was made to do.

Waking up is not fun. You have to get out of your cozy, comfy bed. You have to do stuff. But waking up is how you live. She has been under the covers way too long. Let's wake Her up!

My 100 days of *Being Me on Purpose* didn't come from a book. There were no steps that I followed. It was messy and miraculous, humbling and exhilarating. One of the days, I asked myself where I could be useful and she whispered, *Write your stories.* I wrote them not knowing why.

Then another day, she whispered, *Share your stories.* I publicly shared a few stories. I watched my sharing give other women curiosity and permission to find themselves. One day, she said that I was going to write a book. When I asked Her, *Why are we writing this book?* She said, *You'll see, just write it.* When I told Her that I was scared and didn't feel like it would matter, she said, *That's okay, write it anyway.*

Scared and not understanding why, not knowing what or who it was for, I wrote the book. This is not a workbook or a new thing to add into your routine or change. I share my stories to open the curtains and let the light shine on your life. Maybe some of my experiences will awaken you to your new day. Maybe you need me to drag your ass out of bed to show you that **YOU** exist!

Knowing Her will light up every aspect of your life. Your relationships will be more fulfilling and more stable. Your career will have more meaning and direction. Your ability to be useful in difficult circumstances will increase. Your love and admiration for yourself will be enough, enough for you to pour out to everyone around you.

This is my journey of finding Her, getting to know Her, and striving to get out of Her way. Let's start your journey. Let's find you.

She's been under the covers far too long. It is a new day, and the world is waiting. **WAKE HER UP!**

# WAKE HER UP

# CHAPTER 1

## LIVING ASLEEP

*I didn't know I was asleep until I woke up. When did I fall asleep? What did I miss?*

*"You're back," she said. "How long have I been out?" I asked. "Years, I haven't seen you like this since before you were married, when you lived in New York."*

*I had been married for nine years.*

*It was my first summer being divorced.*

*Most of those nine years were happy. Well, I was happy, and thought he was too. I had built a few businesses. We had two healthy kids. I put him through law school. We moved and bought a forever home. I was doing it. I was doing life, how everyone said to do it. Life was good. Everything was fine.*

*If I never wake up, am I really alive?*

### Where Are You?

The air was warm and the water chill. The spray from the waterfall ran across my face as it poured down the mossy cliff. **HORRIFIC** pain surged through my body, but it didn't seem to pertain to me. I smelled the flowers and could taste the salt in the air. Any moment, a monkey could swing through the luscious trees that filled my view. Another surge of pain roared through me, but I didn't need to do anything about it. I floated in the water and focused on my breathing.

"**PUSH**! The baby is here," she demanded. I pushed as I floated under the waterfall. When I opened my eyes, they put her in my arms. There she was, my first baby girl. I was in a hospital surrounded by nurses and doctors. There was no waterfall, no luscious trees, no salty air. There was blood and harsh lighting. I had birthed a baby and dreamed through it.

I had learned the practice of Hypnobirthing in preparation for my first child's birth. Practicing self-hypnosis through visualization and relaxation techniques to reduce my fear and allow my body to naturally birth my baby. The power to remove myself from overwhelming pain has served me well. But just as intentionally getting a good night's sleep can serve you, sleeping day in and day out will destroy you.

We can get a lot done and not actually be awake. We can push babies out while we sleep. We can make meals for years, do endless dishes, finish a million loads of laundry, build businesses, have relationships, buy houses, have jobs, all while being unaware that we aren't actually there.

## The Only Way

I grew up with my Mom being home and Dad going to work. Mom did all the *"good mom"* things; made dentist appointments, helped with school projects, made Halloween costumes, volunteered for PTA, made cookies for neighbors, and served in the church. She canned peaches and salsa, made fresh bread, and fed us every meal. She planned baby showers and went to her monthly book club. My mom was a super mom. She was everything I thought moms should be. And everything I knew I should strive to become.

Most of my friends' families functioned the same way. And those that didn't, it seemed sad. Sad that their mother had to go to work. Sad that their Dad didn't live with them. I learned that the goal was to have the mom home full-time. If you went to college, it was as a backup, just in case your husband died.

My environment told me that a good mother did whatever it took to be at home with her children. Stories at church would tell of families that sacrificed and budgeted to keep the mother home. Being home ensured that children were raised properly. Raising children would provide the ultimate amount of purpose and joy available to a woman. It was our divine nature. In social settings, women asked other women what their husbands did for work, and I watched as they each took pride in their answers. They talked about their children's progress and complained about the daily tasks.

This was Mom life. It's all I ever knew that I should strive to be. When I went to my friends' houses, their Mom would be doing the same things—doing laundry or dishes—making dinner, helping with homework. This was the life that was my fate. It would fulfill my purpose. Being a wife, having children, and being a homemaker would be my highest calling in life. It was what women were meant to do.

This belief was greatly challenged when I became a nanny at 19 and met a new kind of *"good mom."*

After a bad breakup in college, I freaked out and called a Nanny agency. Within a few weeks, I was on a plane headed to New York City.

I found myself 3,000 miles from home, left with the car keys and a hand-drawn map to pick Jill and Henry up from school. I was in the mother role. I knew how this went. I made cookies, did the laundry, and folded clothes while watching the Today Show. I swept the floors, scheduled play dates and dentist appointments.

I started a walking group with the other mothers on the block and got involved with the church. I was doing it!

I decided to step up my game and implement kid chores. I folded all of Jill's laundry and asked her to put it away. She didn't. So, the next day, I left a reminder for her on a sticky note. She still didn't put them away. The clothes sat there for three days until my boss, her Mom, asked to talk to me. I thought she would be so impressed with my efforts to be a good mother. She asked me why her daughter's clothes hadn't been put away. I simply said, "because she hasn't done it." She replied, "I pay you to put them away. Please be sure it gets done tomorrow." I was crushed and confused. *How was I supposed to be a good mother if I couldn't teach them how my mother had taught me?*

The next day, I put the clothes away while being bothered that she didn't see how this was doing her children a disservice. *How would Jill learn any responsibility if she couldn't even put her own clothes away?* I asked Jill how she felt about being 14 and not knowing how to do her own laundry. She said she didn't need to know. "But, what about when you go to college?" I asked her. She said, "There are laundry services for that. And then, when I have my child, I will have a nanny." And from the mouth of a teenager who may have simply thought she was too cool to do laundry, my eyes were opened to the possibility that there wasn't only one way to be a *"good Mom."*

I was not the mom. I was the Nanny. Her mom went to work every day. She had an executive office in the city. She had a black car pick her up for business trips. She came home in the evening and enjoyed dinner with her family. Dinner time was infused with new vocabulary words and everyone sharing about their day. Cookies were not homemade. There was no book club to attend. No late nights at the sewing machine. She attended sports events as often as she was available. And yet, her children were good people. They worked hard and had good grades. There was love and compassion. She was a great mom. The mom seemed fulfilled and happy. And her children were wonderful people. Her home was a welcoming place of peace and comfort.

*How could this be? There wasn't only one way to be a good mom? You could go to work, have someone do your laundry, and pick your kids up from school, and everyone could still be happy? What is this world? Did people back home know about this? Did they know that you could go to work and still be a wonderful mother? You could make cookies ONCE... ONCE a year or not at all and your kids would still love you.*

My eyes had been opened. I woke up to the reality that there was more than one way of being a good mom.

This mother intentionally chose to go to work. She chose to have a nanny and a housekeeper. She didn't apologize for it, or do it out of shame. She chose to raise her children this way. I asked the daughter, "Don't you wish your Mom was home? Don't you miss her?" She said "No. What would she do all day?" This was her life; she didn't know anything else. She loved her life. She had happy, loving parents. Her home was comfortable, and her parents provided everything she needed. She had opportunities I had never been exposed to. At 14-years-old, she talked about college and had a SAT tutor. They went on family vacations and spent all summer at camp with friends.

I believed that if I didn't choose to be a stay-at-home-mom, I would feel guilty and that my children would become lost. This was not what was happening here. Everyone was thriving. They were all good people, loving, kind, friendly, attentive, hard-working, and happy.

It was the opposite of what I knew, yet it wasn't wrong.

There wasn't a way that was worse or better than the other. My mother created thriving children. She created a welcoming home of comfort and love. She provided experiences that were unique to her. Just as the New York mother was doing. Not one was better than the other. They were both creating wonderful lives. I didn't know that a happy mother and home could exist outside of what I was taught.

I was having an awakening. My mind was becoming aware of new ways a woman could find true fulfillment. I could hear birds chirping new possibilities of happiness.

Waking up in the morning just happens. The sun comes up, and it's morning every single day. How do you summon the sun to come up inside yourself? How do you spark a new day from the inside?

You start by noticing the possibility of a new day. A new way of thinking. A new way of reacting. A new way of loving. A new way of **BEING**.

A simple question to ask yourself - **WHAT IF?**

What if my way of being happy isn't your way of being happy?

What if the right way to do life for myself is different from your right way?

What if what brings me joy, wouldn't bring you joy?

What if when you're doing things differently, they aren't wrong.

What if your right way to live, isn't my right way to live?

What if your way to love, isn't my way to love?

What would noticing look like in your life?

If you are going to live, you're going to have to wake up.

*Rain on a Saturday!!*
*I'm going back to bed.*

**MY PERFECT SATURDAY**

6 a.m. - 5-mile run

8 a.m. - Garden and breakfast for the kids

10 a.m. - Son's football game

Noon - Quick lunch

1 p.m. - Home projects

6 p.m. - Babysitter and date

7 p.m. - Dinner and a local concert

11 p.m. - Netflix and snuggle

**HIS SATURDAY:**

Tage spent his Saturdays watching as many documentaries as possible. Coloring for hours with Jane. Eating a bowl of cereal at noon as breakfast and taking a nap on the couch. Then, another documentary. Putting the kids to bed, popping popcorn and then Netflix. *He was obviously doing Saturdays WRONG!*

This was not how Saturdays were supposed to go. *How could he possibly feel good about doing Saturday this way?* This type of Saturday would create total agony within myself. It would feel like a waste of a day to me. Many weekends have been spent with me trying to save him from the agony that I assume comes from spending Saturdays this way. I wanted him to be happy, and therefore he would need to do Saturday in a way that created happiness. What I didn't understand was that I thought my happiness was how everyone found happiness.

Until I heard someone say,

*Other people are not a messed-up version of you.*

His Saturday might not be a messed-up version of my Saturday. A rainy day isn't a messed-up version of my Saturday. What if Tage actually enjoyed his Saturdays? Maybe his happy is different than my happy. Maybe my idea of what Saturday should be isn't the only way. Maybe other ways aren't wrong. Maybe his Saturday is precisely right for him. Maybe joy could still exist on a rainy day.

I've had so many years of arguing about how Saturdays are supposed to go, I've created resentment and frustration. And so many hours of annoyance. All the while my idea of the perfect Saturday was in the way of having a wonderful Saturday.

It took a willingness to open my eyes and see that I was judging how he did Saturday. It took awareness that my frustration was a result of not getting my way. My Saturdays became drastically better after my awakening. I didn't read a book on how to do Saturday. I didn't listen to a podcast or pull up *"Perfect Saturday"* on Pinterest. I simply opened my eyes to a new day... literally.

Awareness allowed us to reinvent Saturdays. What if there was no right way to do Saturday? What would a Saturday look like if we had no idea what a Saturday *should* look like? What would we do? Now we try to invent Saturdays that are best for our family. And when he does his thing on Saturday, I can appreciate that he is doing Saturday exactly right for him.

It takes awareness to realize it's morning. Before you even open your eyes, you ask yourself questions. Do you have to pee? Are you cold? Is your alarm going off? Maybe to notice a new day within yourself it takes the same thing. Start asking questions and noticing that it's a new day, within yourself.

What does she like?

What is bothering her?

What is causing fear?

What brings her joy?

When's the last time she felt awake and alive?

# WAKE HER UP

## CHAPTER 2

# NO MORE BLANKY

*My blanky was a white and yellow checkered, silky quilt tied with yellow yarn. It was attached to me from birth through kindergarten. My youngest girl now has her own blanky. She has snuggled holes through it. When school started, she didn't know how she would live without it.*

*Blankies make us feel safe. They bring us comfort and security. We think we need them. Yet, here we are without our blankets. We aren't walking around the grocery store sucking our thumbs with them. We have learned to live without them.How many things do we have that we can't imagine living without?*

*What is holding us back from unconditional comfort and security? It's hard to imagine a life without your blanky when that's all you've ever known.Sometimes, the thing that is in our way has been there for so long, we haven't ever asked what life would be like without it.*

### No More Buttons

I own the family business, *Love Woolies*. We make mittens and other cozy accessories from old wool sweaters. Years ago, I couldn't see that the tiny buttons on the mittens were keeping us from a drastic increase in productivity.

I was standing at a Farmer's Market one summer selling mittens. *Yup, summer and mittens, I know ... it's a tough sell. That's not the point.* A customer shared with me how she adored her mittens and loved them even more after taking the buttons off. Having the buttons removed allowed her to roll the cuff up under her coat sleeve. It was driving her crazy to have her coat cuff hit her mitten cuff. So, she cut the buttons off and rolled the mitten cuffs up under her coat sleeve.

*Wait, what?! My mom had been sewing buttons on every single mitten for six years, and this lady had the audacity to take them off?! And loved them even more?! How could this be?* No one had ever told me that it was annoying to have the mitten cuff hit the coat cuff.

It felt like someone was taking my blanky. *Nope! We have to have buttons. That's how the mittens have always been.*

Later, during that same market, a new customer was admiring the mittens. She asked if the buttons could come off... *REALLY?!*

I could've ignored it. I could've thought they were wrong, and didn't know anything about mittens. I could've gone as far as thinking they didn't appreciate all the work that had gone into putting buttons on every individual mitten. But, I didn't. I dared to consider... *What if there were no buttons?* I realized I was also annoyed that the cuff of my coat would hit the cuff of the mitten. This solution had never occurred to me. It would be nice to roll it up underneath my coat.

*Hmm, but all sweater mittens everywhere have buttons. That's just how it is. That's how it's always been. How could we just take them off? What would people say?*

My parents had recently passed the family business onto me. They had driven from Utah to California to pick up an industrial button machine so that my mom wouldn't have to hand sew hundreds of buttons. It weighed a ton, and I recently had it carried to my basement by my husband and his friends. I spent hours sorting buttons into pairs. Every week a new batch of mittens would come back from a seamstress. I would carefully select the perfect pair of buttons to go with the mittens. Then, I would sit at the loud button machine sewing buttons on for hours. The fan was cold, I had to bundle up to sit at the machine. The buttons were a labor of love and great sacrifice. The process took time, and was a necessary characteristic of the mittens. *How could I just not put them on?* Plus, this was my parent's thing, I couldn't just change it so drastically after they had driven to California to get the machine and given it to me. And there was the question of what to do with thousands of buttons!?

I ran the idea past Mom and Dad. Mom said, "No way, you can't do mittens without buttons."

I couldn't get over the fact that two customers in one day had told me that they preferred the mittens without buttons. I decided to be brave, break all the rules, and make a batch of mittens with no buttons! I took the mittens to a market. I had prepared for all the conversations about no buttons. I expected sadness, disappointment, and outright protests to the naked mittens. Sale after sale, no one said anything about the missing buttons. And for the past eight years, no one has ever opposed the buttonless mittens.

We reduced our production rate  by 2 weeks. Added an extra feature of rolling the cuff up under your coat for additional warmth. No more sitting at the freezing button machine. No more tediously matching the perfect type of button to the mittens. I donated all the buttons to an elementary school and a preschool teacher. No buttons created an efficiency that I had never imagined.

How long are we going to hold on to our blankies? I could've easily stayed doing buttons never knowing the benefits. I could've been grumpy about my husband's wrong Saturdays for the rest of my life. I could've stayed believing that weekly cookies were a requirement for being a good mom. We have been snuggled up with our blanky for so long, we have no idea what we are missing.

⫷⫷⫷⫷⫷⫷⫷⫷⫷⫷⫷⫷⫷⫷⫷⫷⫷⫷⫷⫷⫷⫷⫷⫷⫷⫷⫷⫷⫷⫷⫷⫷⫷

*"Your way is in your way."*

⫷⫷⫷⫷⫷⫷⫷⫷⫷⫷⫷⫷⫷⫷⫷⫷⫷⫷⫷⫷⫷⫷⫷⫷⫷⫷⫷⫷⫷⫷⫷⫷⫷

I had a whole list of why I shouldn't take the buttons off, and those are just buttons! Imagine the list we create to hold onto things such as our daily soda run. Most of us have a blanky of social media scrolling. Do you have a food blanky? You know when you're sad, or have any feelings at all, you grab your food blanky. Some have shopping blankies. We have piles of blankies, and we wonder why we don't feel alive. We feel consumed, overwhelmed, and invisible. Well yeah, we are under a pile of blankets and terrified to live without them. What would the world feel like without our blankies? **WE DON'T NEED OUR BLANKIES ANYMORE!**

## Food Addict

Three days into my meal plan, I bailed with my daughter's left-over peanut butter and jelly sandwich. As I ate it, I screamed at myself to put it down. I yelled at myself. *You're such a disappointment, why do you do this?* I watched myself open the pantry and get the Oreos out to drown out the yelling. The yelling stopped as I hurried the cookies into my mouth. I stopped at four cookies, because five would be disgusting. As I put them away, I saw the crackers. I hurried and closed the pantry and walked upstairs. I sat in the bathroom and cried.

*Why can't I freaking stick to the meal plan? Okay, no more cookies ever. Look at what it does to you. You can't keep doing this!* I wrote on the mirror, **Day 1 NO SUGAR.** I made a chart and a plan of how many pounds I was going to lose before my birthday. I wrote out meal plans and a new grocery list.

Thirty minutes later, I remembered that box of crackers in the pantry. They had been there for a while. No one was going to eat them. There was only a half sleeve left. I decided that I should just eat them, so I wouldn't think about them anymore. I walked down the stairs into the pantry, got the crackers out and ate them one by one, as I looked forward to tomorrow when I would stick to my meal plan.

The next day came, and I accidentally slept in. My daughter was sick and had to stay home from school. It was going to be a snuggly day on the couch. A snuggly day wasn't complete without a bowl of ice cream. I guess my meal plan would start tomorrow.

This was my life since I can remember. This was my relationship with food. It would yell at me until I ate it, and then I would yell at myself for eating it. If I wasn't eating it, I was yelling at myself to not eat it. By the end of the day, I was so exhausted from resisting that I generally would eat the forbidden food.

I was done beating myself up. To love and accept my body, I hired a personal trainer. Focusing on getting strong and healthy was going to be better than shaming myself into being skinny.

We started doing intense workouts with a group of other girls. I was all in. A few weeks into the program, I was doing more push-ups than anyone and could see the possibility of doing a pull-up. Then the trainer gave us all a meal plan. *Great, bring it on.*

On Day 3, I bailed into three bowls of cereal which led to pizza, which lead to ice cream.

The next morning during our workout, my friend said, "Welp, I totally bailed on the meal plan yesterday." I laughed and said,

"Me too." She said, "Yeah, I had half a snickers bar, so I just skipped dinner."

My brain exploded. *Half a snickers bar, how is that possible? And then skip dinner. I could not comprehend the ability to do that.* That is when I knew my reaction to food was not normal. I physically and emotionally could not have one cookie or some M&M's or half a candy bar. Any of that would lead to something else and then something else.

The very next day after this new awareness, a friend posted on Facebook about how she had found peace with food. She explained how she had been practicing a food addiction recovery program and had not eaten sugar or flour for over three years. She was thrilled about the weight loss but even more thrilled that food wasn't yelling at her anymore.

I had never heard anyone describe what I had been experiencing. *Food addiction was that a real thing?* My soul lit on fire, and I knew that this was the direction I had to go. I cried in horror as if I had been given a life-long diagnosis.

I didn't want to be an addict of any kind. Addicts are horrible humans who steal from people and can't get jobs. Addicts are the people living in the park with cardboard signs asking for money. I could not be an addict.

*How would I tell my husband that I was going to go to an addiction recovery meeting? And then, if I did, how could I ever justify eating my mom's oatmeal cookies ever again?*

I hated everything about this realization. Through tears and torment, I got myself in the car and drove to a recovery meeting.

I slowly found my way through the program. I found a sponsor that helped me work through the 12 steps, twice. I was abstinent from sugar and flour for three years. When I work my program, the food is silent. I have had the privilege to sponsor other addicts and watch the miracle of recovery in their lives.

Through the 12 steps, I have mended relationships and gotten to know myself. Feeling feelings is something I didn't know how to do. I didn't even know I wasn't feeling feelings. The power of letting go is something I've learned to practice on a daily basis. That was over three years ago. The road was not easy, but I can confidently say that I am a recovering food addict.

I have to practice not picking up my addictive foods every day. It is my comfort blanky. Just as you would tell your child, "It's time to put your blanky down. You're a big kid now."

It's time! You're a big girl now.

Dare to notice the blankies you hold. Find the support you need to be able to put your blanky down!

**Visit MarcellaHill.com for resources to food addiction recovery.**

## Smelling Smoke

My grandpa passed away from leukemia. I was sad and would miss him for the rest of my life. I left it at that. I didn't know that I had slowly pulled up the covers of anger and resentment.

I was angry that he had died. I couldn't change it. *Why was I angry? What was really going on?*

After my grandpa passed, I thought my grandma would travel and visit me more often. I imagined great adventures together. I had hoped she would find new talents, passions, and time.

Since I was in high school, she had sent me an envelope every week with coupons, recipes from the newspaper, and a $5 bill. Sometimes an extra $1 from grandpa. She called and sang to me on my birthday every year. She sent boxes of random stuff for holidays. She was wonderful, and I looked forward to being a part of her new chapter.

After my grandpa passed, everything my grandma had been went with him. She didn't travel, and there were no fun trips or visits. She spent more time in her house and forgot my birthday. There were no more coupons or envelopes.

I thought I was angry about my grandpa dying. I thought I was angry at cancer for taking my grandpa. But when I was willing to see what was actually going on, I was angry that things didn't go my way. I was angry that I didn't get my grandma the way I wanted her.

It was horrifying to realize how my anger had gotten in the way of caring for and loving my grandma during a time that she needed me. The anger had kept me from sending my grandma a package. It had kept me from calling her to check in with her. It had kept me from treating her how she had always treated me. Cancer happens, death happens, and there is nothing we can do about it. But now that I was aware of my angry blanket, I could rip it off and show up for my grandma.

As scary as it was to realize I had been so selfish, I'm grateful I saw it. It's seeing it that gave me the ability to choose differently.

What if you were sleeping under a big cozy stack of blankets with ear plugs, an eye mask and just dreaming away? You start sensing something's not right, but you're so cozy in all those blankets. Then you smell the smoke. You're terrified to poke your head out to see what's happening, because what if the house is on fire?

If you aren't willing to see what's actually going on outside of the covers, you risk not living. You risk not saving others. It is scary to see the flames. But it is seeing the flames that gets you out alive. It is seeing the fire that allows you to act and get everyone else out safely.

If you stay under the covers, you risk your life along with everyone around you.

My grandpa was a firefighter, so this analogy seems fitting for a story that made me aware of his wife. I can't save her from her dementia. I can't bring my grandpa back. What I can do, is I can choose to live outside the covers and love and care for her without resentment or anger.

There is a lot in life that is out of your control. But just as a fire can be out of control, you have the ability to get out alive and create a whole new life.

Do you dare take the covers off? Do you dare smell the smoke and see the flames? Do you dare to allow yourself to get out and live?

# WAKE HER UP

# CHAPTER 3

# OPEN YOUR EYES

*It's hard to see what's right in front of you if your eyes are closed. Until you open your eyes, you will stay in that place between sleeping and being awake.*

*Not knowing what's real, not truly living. You're going to have to open your eyes.*

*Grandpa Jack*

Chris and I had just moved to a tiny town. We were renting the cutest little yellow house. The owners told us to stay out of the way of the old man next door. He hated Mormons and was really mean.

Most mornings, he was in his front yard picking up sticks from the nightly wind. With an annoyed demeanor, he would also pick up sticks in my yard. I imagined him thinking that my yard was a mess. *He must think that I'm lazy and inconsiderate to leave all the branches laying on my lawn for him to pick up.*

When the kids were being loud in the backyard, I could hear him on the other side of the fence. He was probably just waiting for us to reach a certain noise level so he could say something or just complain to his wife about us. He never introduced himself. He never smiled. He was a mean old man that hated us.

After several months of avoiding this mean old man, I parked in front of our house on the street and went around the other side to get my kids out of the car. The grumpy old man was right next to my car picking up sticks, just trying to make a point that I had a messy yard. I got my 3-year-old out and, without any notice, she walked up to him and put her arms up. I held my breath. He picked her up. *Oh No!* And then, she hugged him. My heart stopped. The mean old man melted right in front of me. He dropped the stick and hugged her back. He lit up and smiled with his whole being. I eventually found my breath and the words, "Good afternoon." Then, he asked her name, our names, and where we were from. He asked if I needed any help getting the groceries to the house.

Every morning from then on, when I would get home from the gym, he would be out picking up sticks and would ask if I had worked hard enough. I'd laugh and give him a hard time for not being there. If I missed a few days, he would be out front telling me that he was getting worried. He would peak over the fence when we were playing in the back yard and ask what all the ruckus was all about. We brought him cookies and the kids made him homemade trinkets. He invited us over to watch the Olympics on his big screen TV, and showed us all his new technology that he was so proud of.

It wasn't true. He was never a grumpy old man. He was never judging me. He was never thinking that I had an awful yard. He never thought I was lazy or inconsiderate. He was looking for a friend. He was trying to be a sweet old man. He was our Grandpa Jack.

Writing this, my heart still misses him as if he was my real grandpa. Oh, what I would've missed had my eye mask stayed on. The owners had given me an eye mask. I put it on and never thought to take a look for myself.

Eye masks are passed out as if they are doing us a favor. Our parents, friends, community, and culture have all told us what to believe and how the world should be. Have you ever asked yourself how the world should be? Have you ever dared take the eye mask off and see what is actually going on?

What if no one told you how to be a good mom?

What if no one told you how to have a good marriage?

What if no one told you what a sexy body looked like?

What if no one told you how to be successful?

What if no one told you who you are supposed to be?

Allow yourself to take the eye mask off.

Imagine... all the possibilities.

## Going to Hell

I found myself in a nightmare of shame driving home one morning after having sex with a man I barely knew.

Divorced, lonely, and starved for affection, I found myself in the company of a man that wanted me. All I knew of dating was from high school and college. Coming from a religious up-bringing, I was taught that premarital sex was a sin as serious as murder. I thought that people that had sex out of wedlock must have lost their faith in God, and had hit rock bottom in their spiritual lives.

I had been on a spiritual high. I was reading my scriptures more than ever. I was clinging to my prayers and going to the temple as often as possible. I felt closer to God than I had ever been. *How could I abandon everything I believed in? How could I betray myself like this?* I believed I had made sacred covenants with God to be morally pure. The consequence for breaking those covenants was hell. *I was evil.*

*How did this happen?* We went out on a few dates, he was comfortable, he was sweet, and he really liked me. I didn't want to be alone. I didn't want to sleep alone. I had slept with another person in my bed for nine years. So, I started sleeping over. There was never a conscious decision to take things to the next level. It just happened. *I had premarital sex! I had basically committed murder. I was going straight to hell...* or so I thought.

*I was a horrible person. How could I face my parents? How would I go about being a good mother? I must have been kidding myself that I was close to God. No one would do this if they were close to God.* As I drove home from his house needing to get my kids breakfast and ready for the day, I was in complete disgust of myself. *How could I even dare to walk in that house and call myself a mother? I was dirty and had just destroyed my entire existence.*

(Wow, we can really destroy ourselves over a 10-minute drive.)

Through tears and desperation, I thought enough to call my therapist, and by some miracle she answered.

I sat in my parent's driveway not knowing how to get my wretched self out of the car. I explained to my therapist what I had done, and that I was now going to hell. She asked, "Are you in hell right now?" I said, "No."

"Well, surprise! You don't go to hell. You are an adult that has the ability to choose a responsible sexual relationship. You are still a good mother. You are still a good daughter. You are still you. You can even still talk to God. You are still useful. You are still a benefit to society. Your existence makes the world a better place. If you choose that this is not what brings you happiness, then you can make other choices. But right now, you have not gone to hell. Right now, you have children and parents who love you, and you can keep showing up for them." She said.

She woke me up to what was real. Maybe I do go to hell, but in that moment, I had kids who needed their mother, and they deserved a happy, healthy, unashamed mother.

In a nightmare of shame, I would've had a day of hiding in my bedroom. I would have been unworthy of smiles or any joy. I would have taken moments to cry in disgust of myself. No eye contact would've been made. My nightmare would've consumed all of me and all of my interactions. I would no longer be available for what was real.

Gratefully, I was told that shame was unnecessary. Not only unnecessary, but incredibly harmful to myself and my children. It wasn't having sex that would cast me into darkness. It was the nightmares of shame, fear, resentment, doubt, and self-destruction that would've made me disappear.

I chose to see the truth and be a happy, present mother. I was able to think more clearly and make conscious decisions on what I wanted to do with my relationship with Tage. *Was I a desperate, hot mess? Yes! Did I make stupid decisions that I wish I had done differently? Of course!* But that does not make the nightmare of being cast down to hell true.

I made a lot of choices out of pain and fear during that time in my life. Yet the decision to not live in a nightmare of shame is a choice that allowed me to live and be available to myself and my children.

Do you wake up to the same thing every day? The same resentments, the same complaints, the same self-talk? Can you hear yourself screaming inside? It's the same bad dream over and over and over and over.

Let's wake Her up and get Her out!

4 4 4 4 4 4 4 4 4 4 4 4 4 4 4 4 4 4 4 4 4 4 4 4 4 4 4 4 4 4 4 4 4 4 4 4 4 4 4 4 4 4 4

*"What would you be without the thought?"*

— BYRON KATIE

4 4 4 4 4 4 4 4 4 4 4 4 4 4 4 4 4 4 4 4 4 4 4 4 4 4 4 4 4 4 4 4 4 4 4 4 4 4 4 4 4 4 4

## Mean Girls

The mean girls were in 5th grade, the Angela's. Side pony-tails with bright-colored scrunchies. Gerbaud jeans, high-top sneakers, and as many New Kids on the Block watches that would fit. They were the prettiest, coolest girls in school. Sometimes they were my friends, and sometimes not. At recess, they made up a dance routine on the swings to the song, *Don't Worry, Be Happy*. They took all the swings for the entire recess. With their matching shirts, they sang while swinging in sync. I watched and memorized.

After school, I practiced the routine with my sister. Just in case, someday, I was honored enough to be in their club, I'd be ready to step in. That day never came.

On a lucky Friday, they invited me to a sleepover birthday party. I had made it! I was in the club! I was one of the cool girls. I must have finally become pretty enough to be their friend. Until the next morning when, at breakfast, they served me my training bra on a plate. They froze it overnight. Everyone thought it was hilarious. I was mortified. Pretty sure I just went along with it to save my dignity, but I knew that I wasn't really in their club.

I wasn't cool enough. I wasn't pretty enough. I was a joke.

Another time, we were all at the pool, and I thought maybe this time we could all be friends. We played in the pool, and it seemed like it was all going well. We got to the locker room and someone's bra was hung up in the middle of the stalls, and everyone including me was laughing. I went to get changed, and I realized it was mine. I sat in the stall and cried until everyone left. I was not cool. I was a joke.

I finally decided to stop trying to be cool enough to be in their club. I decided to make my own club. I gathered up my friends, and we started the TGI Friday Club. We made matching purple puffy paint t-shirts and wore them to school every Friday. We went to someone's house once a week and did a craft or service project. Fifty cent weekly dues made us an official club.

Looking back, I'm pretty sure we weren't in the *cool* category, but I loved wearing my purple shirt to school with my club. I loved that we all had a place to belong with our scrunchies and matching shirts.

Twenty-five years has gone by since I last spoke to the Angela's. I was tagged in a Girl Scout Facebook photo with them, and suddenly we were connected. One of them reached out and said hello. I said something about feeling like I was never cool enough to be their friend. And she said, "I always thought you were the coolest person."

My heart stopped. I read it over and over and over. I didn't even know how to respond. All this time, I had thought of her as the mean girl, snd she had thought kind things about me. Maybe she had been mean. Maybe we were just kids, and kids can be jerks, but at 40 years old, I still believed that she was the mean girl and that I was just a joke to her. *Now, who was the mean girl?* I wasn't only judging her, but I was also allowing myself to think I was a joke.

Things are, many times, not what we tell ourselves. For the past 25 years, she was not the mean girl, and I was not the joke.

# WAKE HER UP

# CHAPTER 4

# KICK THEM OUT

*You wouldn't get in bed with a mean person. People sleep on the couch all the time because someone was being mean. Mean people do not belong in your bed.*

*Kick them out of your bed and out of your head.*

## The Toy Man

At 26 years old, I stood at my booth in New York City during the International Toy Fair. I was introducing the world to my new toy, the Peek-a-Boo Bag. Our toy was a quiet travel toy. Imagine a large bean bag with a plastic window on the front. It was filled with white beads and 39 different objects to find. *Shake it, Squish it, Find it* was the tagline. There was a toy with part of that tagline as it's actual name. This toy was in all major retail stores. I had admired this company for years. I dreamed of the possibility of working together with our complimentary toys. My booth was just two aisles over from this famous toy company. Throughout the day, I caught glimpses of the man I admired and looked forward to meeting him. Our meeting didn't quite go as I had planned.

I was standing at my booth talking to a buyer. The creator I admired walked up to my booth and interrupted our conversation. He demanded to know my name. His breath was heavy, and he was visibly angry. He asked how long I'd been in business and if I had a patent. He informed me that I was in breach of his patent by using his name and that I needed to immediately stop selling or I was going to hear from his attorney. The potential customers were uncomfortable, yet stayed to ensure my safety. He was red in the face and raising his voice. He said, "Little girl, you are out of your league. You have no idea who you are dealing with. You will be hearing from my attorney."

I imagined security guards coming and walking me out of the Javits center. How embarrassing it would be to have to take my booth down in the middle of the show. *Had I crossed a line? Was I breaking the law?* I just wanted him to like me and my toy. I thought we were going to be friends and maybe collaborate on new ideas. Now, he was threatening me and trying to shut me down.

Maybe I was out of my league. I didn't actually know what I was doing. My booth was homemade with pool noodles and duct tape. I was writing orders down on paper. I hadn't even done my first run of production with our overseas manufacturer. *I probably should just pack up and leave, right?*

After all, this was an owner of a toy that was in Target and Barnes and Noble. He obviously knew what he was doing. I wanted his respect and encouragement. I wanted to apologize and make it right. I wanted him to be wowed by what I had done. *We were going to make such a good team. It was going to be so good...* Or so I thought.

I had no words for a response to his outburst. I felt small and bullied. He eventually walked away. Several customers reassured me that he was being awful and to ignore him. I was still anticipating security showing up any second.

A fellow vendor that had seen the whole thing woke me up to a new reality. He said, "Well, he seemed pretty threatened by your toy. Must mean you've got something pretty great. Isn't this your first time? Most companies on this aisle don't get that much attention. You should be very proud."

I called my husband who had recently finished law school and worked at a patent law firm. I suddenly realized that this guy had no idea who he was dealing with. I had access to the information I needed. We decided it would be best to stay out of this man's way. We got creative and changed our tagline to *Shake it, Squish it, Spot it* which was better anyway because then it was all S's.

What he thought of me wasn't true. I was not a little girl that didn't know what I was doing. I was an entrepreneur that had raised enough funding to manufacture my idea overseas. I was standing in New York City receiving orders. I had the power to make my dreams into reality. I certainly had no use for a mean man to be in my head telling me otherwise.

He was not my customer. He was not the one that was going to buy my toys. If he didn't like my toy, that was okay. If he didn't like me, that was okay too. My customers liked my products. My customers liked me.

As the saying goes... what he thought of me was NONE of my business.

People will disappoint you. They will not be what you expect. The relationship could take a wrong turn. There will be differences of opinion. They simply won't like you. No matter how good you thought it could be, do not get in bed with them! Recognize that it's not going well. Choose to see what is actually happening. Kick them out of your head as quickly as you would your bed.

I had survived the humiliation at the Toy Fair. I had survived the bra jokes in 5th grade. And yet, there was more to learn about other people's opinions being none of my business.

# The Verdict

I worked full-time when Tage and I got married. The hour commute was awful, but the job was wonderful until they started downsizing. I quickly found a job closer to home. It was perfect. A start up—I'd started a few companies myself. Developing a customer service department, which was my prior job with a direct sales company, which I had done for five years. I was made for this position.

It wasn't your typical job application and interview. I asked to spend a day with the team and assess what the needs were. I wrote up a proposal for the job they actually needed and was hired. I was given a company card. Free creative decorating power for our department. I brought in cubicles and helped build a new phone system. We painted and brought in new furniture.

The team grew from three agents to twelve, speaking five different languages. I was passionate about building a company that would make a large global impact. I had no idea that all my experience would lead to this, but I was thrilled. I looked forward to one day being a part of the executive team and inspiring others to fulfill their purpose through this company.

One Thursday, I participated at a regular meeting with all of the executives and department heads. As a start-up, they were still figuring out communication and how to effectively roll out new ideas. I asked a lot of questions to ensure my team had the information they needed. Everything seemed to be going well. I was learning to use my voice thanks to Sheryl Sandberg and her book, *Lean In*.

At the end of the day, I was called into one of the executive's offices. I anticipated a positive conversation about my team's response to recent changes. So, you can imagine my surprise when the first words out of his mouth were, "This will be your last day here, you aren't a good fit."

I was speechless as he handed me my last paycheck. I asked, "Why? What happened?"

He replied, "That right there, that's why. You and that attitude just aren't a good fit for this company anymore."

"I'm confused. Did something happen? Why wouldn't you give me any notice? I'm six months pregnant, I'm the main income for my family, and I've hired incredible people."

The other executive in the room jumped in, "You're the main income in your family?"

I responded, "Yes. Does that make a difference?"

"See, there you go with your flippant attitude. We aren't putting up with that anymore," said the executive, as he pushed himself back in his chair and folded his arms.

They had made up their mind and arguing wasn't going to accomplish anything. Instead of trying to save my job, I immediately stated that if they wanted a *Yes man* then they certainly shouldn't have hired me. They were fully aware that I was coming in to do the job my way, and that it was the basis upon which they had hired me. My last statement was, "If you want a doormat, then you should hire a doormat." That was one of those moments in your life that miraculously you say exactly what you should say and walk out a whole person, if not even more whole than when you walked in.

Having recently read *Lean In* by Sheryl Sandberg, I was surprised to witness firsthand the discrimination she talked about and realizing that it actually exists. Women are still being told they are too aggressive, and that they shouldn't speak up. I had never been aware of it before. Now my life was going to change drastically due to this discrimination.

I figured I'd get unemployment, go on a wonderful vacation, and enjoy having my baby. I'd have time and income to find a new job. I filed for unemployment thinking that would be the end of that. They denied my unemployment. I appealed their denial. We would be going to trial over wrongful termination and sexual discrimination.

I had no idea what was going on. As I worked with a friend that helped me prepare for the trial, I could not come up with anything that they would be able to say against me. The day came and we spent almost four hours in a trial over the phone. They spent about 90 percent of the time tearing apart my character. People that I had called my friends and co-workers, people I had hired and given promotions, friends that I had cried with over their personal life experiences, and mentors who had offered me professional advice and guidance all spoke.

These people, once family from a week ago, now spoke of my awful character and flippant attitude. They told stories that never happened. A girl that I truly loved as a little sister told them that I discriminated against individuals on my team. People I had put my neck out for threw me under the bus.

I didn't have an attorney. I didn't know how to ask questions in a proper legal way. I didn't know that my character would be on trial. I sat alone in my house at the kitchen table watching as they tore me apart and proclaimed to a judge what a horrible human I was. They all did this under oath in a court of law. They used executive's time and paid their attorney to do the work before and during the trial.

Then it was over. I sat at the table beaten and left for dead. *What just happened?* I started the call proud of who I was, and then I sat there not trusting anything that I thought about myself. Surely, if they were going to pay executives to say all those things under oath, there must be some validity to it. *I must not be*

*the person I think I am. Who I think I am must be so far from the truth.*
It broke me.

All I could do was get to my bed and pull the covers up. *I was a worthless human being.* I laid there and just let the terrible things they said eat me up. I thought I would just lay there and wait for the verdict that would prove in a court of law how awful I must be.

I slept through life for a few weeks before the verdict came back.

I flew to see my grandpa for the last time. He was dying of leukemia. The verdict came to my inbox as I was getting off a plane. I sat by myself in the Phoenix airport, with my husband on the phone. My hands shook as I read. I was about to read the verdict of who I truly was.

In writing, from a judge, he stated that they had no basis to fire me. I had done my job to the best of my ability. That I only ever had the company in my best interest. He went on to explain how they had not done their job properly, and he explained how to properly let someone go.

I read it over and over. I wasn't a horrible human. I was worth keeping. I worked hard and cared about the people. I was exactly the woman I thought I was, and they were as wrong as I had hoped they were.

That weekend, I was able to give my best self to the last moments I would spend with my grandpa, with no doubt about who I was.

A few weeks later, the company would appeal the judge's verdict. *You know, because when you are a sexist asshole and a woman wins, you just can't believe it, so you question the judge.* The appeal was in writing. I could've read all of the jabs at my character on paper. Almost five pages long. I didn't read it. My response was two lines long: "I did my job to the best of my ability. My efforts were always in the best interest of the company."

And of course, I won again, but this time I didn't need to win to know who I was. It bothered me that I needed that verdict to know who I was. I should know who I am with or without it. *Why was I so crushed by that trial?*

⫷⫷⫷⫷⫷⫷⫷⫷⫷⫷⫷⫷⫷⫷⫷⫷⫷⫷⫷⫷⫷⫷⫷⫷⫷⫷⫷⫷⫷⫷⫷⫷⫷⫷⫷⫷⫷⫷⫷⫷⫷⫷⫷

### *Mean people don't belong in your bed or your head.*

⫷⫷⫷⫷⫷⫷⫷⫷⫷⫷⫷⫷⫷⫷⫷⫷⫷⫷⫷⫷⫷⫷⫷⫷⫷⫷⫷⫷⫷⫷⫷⫷⫷⫷⫷⫷⫷⫷⫷⫷⫷⫷⫷

## *Bed Bugs*

I had a bad bed bug situation. I was bitten from head to toe after the trial, and yet, I went and got into bed and let them bite me over and over and over. When the verdict came, it killed all the bugs in my head. If you woke up with bites all over you, what would you do?

You would rip off the covers. Possibly burn them. Get a new mattress. Extreme measures would be taken. So why not take some extreme measures to get them out of your head?

Who or what is in your head right now?

What keeps replaying in your mind?

What has been said to you that you keep repeating?

You're too...?

You're not... enough?

We've got to see the mean things.

We've got to find the bugs. That's the only way you'll know why your skin is crawling all the time.

# WAKE HER UP

# CHAPTER 5

# IT'S NOT WORKING, GOING BACK TO BED

*Waking up is not a difficult process. You don't take a class to learn how to wake up. You don't need a manual or special training. Your body just does it. Even when you're not intentionally waking up, you still wake up.*

*When you are trying to wake up your soul, it will feel the same. It's tiny things that can wake you up. Just a cool breeze can bring you from dreaming to awareness. Asking yourself questions won't feel earth shattering, but it all counts. The slightest beam of light will wake you up.*

## Hypnobirthing

I had three babies naturally. No epidural. Not because I'm a superwoman and not because I'm all about being natural, but because my aunt almost died from her epidural, and it seemed more scary to get one than not to. I took a Hypnobirthing class to prepare. They taught us how our bodies were made to have babies. Apparently, your body just knows how to have a baby. They taught us to trust our bodies.

We practiced meditations to allow our bodies to do what they needed to do. This was my first introduction to the idea that my thoughts get in the way of my actual self. A woman came to our home and gave us a brief example of hypnotherapy. She had me close my eyes and imagine a ladder. My mind started sorting through a catalog of ladders, metal ladders, antique ladders, step stools, and glittery ladders ascending to Heaven. So many ladders that I couldn't decide on a ladder! Even as I imagined taking steps up the ladder, the ladder would change. It didn't feel serene; it felt like Home Depot.

She reassured me that through practice I would find the peace and trust that I needed to bring my baby safely into the world. We enrolled in the class.

I practiced hypnobirthing daily. I was determined to learn it. I would turn on the CD and listen to the recording about rainbows. I couldn't make it through the first two colors before falling asleep. Every day, I tried so hard to stay awake, and every time I would wake up with the meditation over. *How was I going to safely bring my child into the world if I could only reach two colors of the rainbow meditation?*

At the next class, the instructor explained how she would test our level of preparedness. She walked us through a meditation and then clamped the top of our hand with a metal alligator clip. She passed it around, and we all looked at it in terror. So sharp, it looked like it would leave me bleeding. I thought, *Oh geez, here we go. I will fake it the best I can.*

She did the meditation and then turned the music off. She asked us to open our eyes and look at our hands. On the top of my hand, there were teeth marks from the alligator clamp. *No way! I had done it? What?! I had done it! I didn't feel it at all!*

I was in my happy space without even knowing it. By just the mere act of trying to find peace and inner strength, I had done it. I wasn't consistent with my practicing. I wasn't even good at it. I'd fall asleep every time. Yet, my effort was enough. Somehow, somewhere, the gap of me trying and missing the mark had been filled. I had the ability in me without even knowing it was there.

Here you are, trying to wake up your soul and feel alive. You're trying to know who you truly are. Just being here counts. Reading this sentence is you trying. You are doing it.

## *Trying counts!*

There is no one way to wake up your soul. There is not a wrong or right way to do this. There has never been a YOU before. Nobody knows exactly how SHE wakes up. SHE is the only one that knows.

You'll have to trust that She was created to live. She knows how to wake up. You just have to get out of Her way.

## Mystery Caller

I had been betrayed by a past employee. She spoke against me during the wrongful termination hearing. She was like a sister to me. She said horrible things. Things that were not true. She was dear to me, and she broke my heart.

Six years had passed. I didn't think of it anymore, until I was doing some inner work and letting go of resentments. Her name came up. I found it odd because it didn't cause me any pain in my day-to-day life. I didn't associate with her or anyone that knew her, and yet there she was on the page.

I thought about what had happened. I thought about what her experience may have been. I asked myself if I could've done anything differently. I could've chosen to not believe what she had said. I could've believed that she was being put in a really tough situation that was most likely threatening her job. I chose to forgive her. I hoped that she was not holding any ill feelings over something that had happened so long ago.

I didn't know how to contact her to tell her that I forgave her. I couldn't find her on Facebook. I wrote her a letter not knowing if I would be able to find her. I talked to God about it and figured that was all I could do.

A week later, I was standing at a Farmer's Market, because I do that a lot, and a girl walked up to me and handed me her phone. She said someone would like to talk to you. The girl handing me the phone was Karen's sister. I had forgotten that she knew my sister, and that she would know that I sell my mittens at the market every Saturday. I looked at the phone and it said Karen. I put the phone to my ear and I had no words. My eyes filled with tears.

She told me how sorry she was for what she had done. She explained how the executives had threatened her job. They had written on a white board how she was to respond during the hearing. She said she should've called sooner. We both cried. I said thank you and was able to shower her with love and forgiveness. I wished her peace and joy in her life.

There was no way that she could've known I was thinking of her, writing about her, and talking about her, and yet all those efforts were enough to accomplish the thing that needed to be done.

How often do we not even try to do something because we have no idea how to actually do it? We can't see how it would be possible. We don't think it matters or would even make a difference. But this, this mattered. It allowed for so much peace and love for both of us.

Try it for yourself.

Pick a resentment. Write it down, look at it. Think about it in a different way than you've ever considered before. Ask questions about it. What would you do differently? Were you being fearful or self-seeking? What might have been their experience? Flip it all around and inside out.

Write it down.

Sit with it.

Then watch and listen. Things will start happening that are beyond explanation. Someone will call. You will read something. The radio will say something that will make you think differently. You'll bump into someone unexpectedly. An entirely new idea will show up. Just wait, listen, and watch.

## Mitten Filing System

Building *Love Woolies* has felt similar to my hypnobirthing experience. Sorting through ladders, trying to choose the best course to take. Doing social media, production, team building, a little here and there, and not knowing if it's doing anything at all. It has been amazing to watch the gap between my trying and not knowing be filled over and over and over.

I was struggling to find an effective inventory system for the mittens. They are all one-of-a-kind. I would sell one and then dig through a bin trying to match the colors to the listing. Bad system. I googled, "How to inventory one-of-a-kind products," and even Google didn't have any suggestions! I was on my own. Not totally alone, I had me, my inner self, and the universe.

In the middle of my office, I stopped and sat on the floor and had a chat with the universe. I spoke out loud, *"If this company is going to grow, I can't be digging through bins every time I get an order. I need some guidance on how to organize my inventory. What I'm doing has never been done."* I sat still and allowed my thoughts to float away. I needed space to find a new idea. I sat and waited in the space of nothing and everything. Watching thoughts and breath flow in and out. I wiggled my toes and resumed my chat, *"I'm going to get up and do something, please accept my trying and guide me."*

I stood up and saw a page of small stickers on the desk. I started writing numbers on the stickers. I noticed the stickers were just the right size to stick on the mitten tags. The visual of filing the mittens in a drawer came to me. I had a long dresser in my office. I started putting the mittens in numerical order like a filing system. I learned how to add the coordinating SKU number to each product online. To this day, we still use the SKU number filing system for all of our one-of-a-kind products.

There was no book. No class. No one to ask. There was only me, my inner self, and the universe. I understood the problem. I had the answer inside of me.

## Showing Up

I felt like I should go visit Kim White. She lived in the neighborhood when she was first diagnosed with cancer. On social media, it appeared she had a lot of support. So many comments, so many followers. She didn't know me, other than as a girl in the neighborhood. I didn't want to get involved and just be another person appearing to want to be in on the drama of her life. I ignored it for hours.

It wouldn't go away. So, I finally made up a bag of random stuff just to be able to look like I had a reason to come by and drop off a gift. I hesitantly drove over. I knocked and no one answered. I went to put the bag down and leave, but then the door slowly opened. She peered out from a dark room. It was apparent that she had been crying.

I casually asked, "How are you?" *Stupid question.* She casually responded, "Fine," while both of us knew that she was clearly not fine. I had the audacity to ask again with a more concerned tone. "But really, Kim, how are you?" And she collapsed in my arms, sobbing uncontrollably. I gathered her frail body in my arms and walked her to the couch.

I sat with her as she poured out all her fear, anger, worry, defeat, and sorrow. No one had come to visit her for days. No one was bringing her family meals. I couldn't believe it. *What if I hadn't come?*

I don't know why out of all the people, in that moment, on that day, I was the one to show up. Maybe lots of people were getting the same feeling but just hadn't shown up yet. I was able to help organize meals for their family and regular visits.

That moment has become a reminder to me to show up even if I don't think it matters. Even when it doesn't make sense. I don't need to justify or reason my actions.

Existing and showing up ... it counts.

## 1-800-Call-Mom

My siblings and I call my mom almost every day. We call for everything from recipes, advice, being bored, depressed, to discuss our annoyances, and just because. She always picks up. She will pick up in the middle of a brunch with friends just to make sure we are okay.

My sister, Sharon, and I were talking about how our mom is like a *mom hotline*. And then our creativity went rampant. *What if there was a Mom Hotline?!* Women who don't have moms could call, and women who don't have children could pick up. People could call to celebrate that they are pregnant or just ask for a good banana bread recipe. They could call when they are devastated and just need someone to tell them it's going to be okay. *Wouldn't that be amazing?* Someone should do that.

My sister has a big following on TikTok *(Sharon.a.life)* and she shared this idea with her audience. The power of social media broke our world open to the overwhelming desperate need to be able to just call Mom.

Comments such as, "I lost my mom three years ago, and then my aunt. I don't have anyone. What I wouldn't give to call my mom again. Please make this happen."

Or, "My mom won't speak to me. I just found out I'm pregnant, and I can't call her. Please make this happen. I want to call someone who cares."

Thousands and thousands of comments begging for this to exist. I read through the comments in tears. I had no idea how many people couldn't pick up the phone to call their mom when I was calling my mom multiple times a day. My heart broke wide open.

I didn't know what to do. *How was I going to start a new project in the middle of writing a book, launching a speaking career, still managing a company, a family, a marriage, and summer was just starting?*

I had no clue how I would make this happen, but I could not ignore it. I did what I could. I popped up a google form so people could enter their information if we were ever to actually make it a real thing. This way we would have emails, and we could get in touch with everyone.

I made a Facebook group to start connecting Mothers and Daughters.

I asked for Mom volunteers to send out texts to the daughters. In one day, 500 women without a mom received a text that said, "Hope you know how wonderful you are. Love a Mom."

It was going to be Mother's Day, and everyone was posting about how difficult Mother's Day was going to be. We organized a Mother's Day card exchange. 250 women sent and received Mother's Day cards.

I tried doing a Kickstarter, but the world wasn't ready for that.

Today the Facebook page still exists, and the feed is filled with posts that start, "Hey Mom"... and then everything from... "Just wanted to tell you I miss you to I graduated today."

It's a place that allows women to love without restraint, love and be loved unconditionally. I had no intention of all this when my sister shared our idea. I didn't think through it or even dream it up. 1-800-Call-Mom just showed up. I could've ignored it. I could've done nothing. I could still leave it at a Facebook group and have that be it.

But me saying yes to showing up where I could has impacted hundreds of women. I don't know why I get a front row seat to this beautiful project, but I'm humbled and amazed to see the power of saying yes and trying.

## *Trying counts.*

**Visit MarcellaHill.com to become a volunteer Mom or Daughter of 1-800-Call-Mom**

# WAKE HER UP

# CHAPTER 6

# RIP OFF THE COVERS

*My husband insists on sleeping with the fan on. As if getting up in the morning wasn't already difficult. I know as soon as I take the covers off, the chilly air is going to hit me. I sleep in sweats and a sweatshirt year-round. I hate the cold. There is no way around it. In order to live out in the world, you have to remove the covers. It's going to be uncomfortable.*

## A New Way of Being

Joe sent his old sweater to *Love Woolies*. He purchased it in Switzerland, while serving with the Coast Guard. The sweater was cherished and worn for several years until it ended up on a shelf in the closet. When he went to wear it again, moths had gotten to it. He found Love Woolies, and asked if we could make mittens from his beloved sweater.

After seeing over 50,000 sweaters, I know what a rare, extra special sweater looks like, and Joe's was beyond anything I had ever seen. It was red and white with snowflakes. The detail in the knit was exquisite. It had been loved and cherished. Aside from a few moth holes, it was still in wonderful condition. It felt wrong to purposely shrink it and cut it up.

The sweater had served its purpose as a sweater, and now it was time for it to become something more. In order to do that, we had to wash it and cut it up. It was not easy to put Joe's sweater into the hot water. It felt as if I was washing away all the memories. Transferring it to the dryer, I knew there was no turning back. His sweater would never be the same. It would never be a sweater ever again.

Shrunken and still intact, it laid on the cutting table, awaiting its fate. I took the blade and cut the arms off, then separated the front from the back. I laid the pattern down and cut out the pieces for mittens. This beautiful sweater with so many memories was now in several different pieces. Useless at the moment. Unrecognizable from what it had been.

I lovingly designed it with other coordinating pieces. Creativity was poured into it, hoping that it would become more than it had ever been. I sent it off to be sewn by one of our incredibly talented seamstresses, and a week later it came back.

I opened the box and took out the mittens. As I held them in my hands and turned them over and over, they were the greatest pair I had ever seen. They were new, and Joe's sweater was alive and well. His sweater would once again give warmth and memories in a way it had never imagined.

We auctioned off the mittens for charity, and the mittens made from Joe's sweater are now adored and loved by three new owners, one being Joe's wife, who bought a pair as a surprise for Joe.

Finding purpose requires discomfort. A rearranged version of yourself creates a new reality. Out of the covers is a new way of being. We are cozy and warm under those covers of fear, resentment, and regret. We have convinced ourselves that this is it, we just have to learn how to be okay with it. It can be painful and scary to rearrange yourself.

Maybe you feel like Joe's sweater... Hidden away under a pile of uselessness for years, wanting life to go back to the way it was. It's unfixable. You are not meant to be fixed. You have the ability to create a new existence again and again.

In the Love Woolies workshop, above the damaged sweaters, a sign reads:

*The world is no longer happening to you,*
*You were meant to happen*
*to the world.*

## Torn Up Beyond Recognition

"It's almost too good to be true," I wrote in my journal just one month before finding out about the affair. I felt whole and complete. We were serving our true purpose during that season in our life. I had no reason to cut it open. I didn't know I was under the covers.

He had recently finished law school. Our new house was more than I had ever imagined. Living close to his family provided cousins and sisters. I expected to live in a big city, but the vast land and prairies that stretched to the horizon filled my soul.

We purchased our forever home with endless projects to make it our own. We were both youth leaders in our church. Wednesday evenings we hosted youth waffle parties. Long days were spent in the garden with the kids running in nothing but a diaper or jammies. Fresh paint and new floors, the sweat and sacrifice of scraping popcorn ceilings had literally been scraped into our home. A beautiful banister greeted you as you entered the front door. This was it, our forever home, our cute babies, our crazy dog, a big garden, and everything we had ever wanted.

He started a band with his brothers. I started a preschool from our home. Couponing and canning salsa with kids under toe. He played basketball and wrote music. *How does it get better than this?*

And then slowly, like a snag in your favorite sweater, our beautiful life started to unravel. I noticed them talking at church. I saw his truck driving away from her house during his lunch break. Wasn't totally strange though, as we were all friends. We had been camping together. Our kids were friends. We helped each other with home projects. At first it just felt like I was crazy and making things up out of my own insecurities.

I'd say something to point out my concern, and he'd apologize that it appeared that way, and we would move on. Snag fixed. But then there would be another and another.

I tried to put it back together. We went to therapy. We had endless talks to try and mend the brokenness. I thought *we* were trying to fix it. Then, in the middle of trying to fix what he had done, he said, "You're just too much. It's embarrassing to go anywhere with you. Everyone always wants to talk to you. Why can't I ever be enough?"

I hadn't realized until he said this, that I had made myself so small to make him comfortable. If I made myself any smaller, I would disappear. I had been muting myself out. I had smashed myself into a tiny box of trying to be a good wife and a good mother to ensure his happiness. I wanted to be selfless and not get in his way. I thought if I did everything right, he would be happy and then *we* would be happy.

I thought he was proud of my outgoing personality. My drive and ambition were parts that made me shine. My favorite parts of me were too much for him; they were the parts he had come to hate.

That comment ripped me apart far more than the affair. It rearranged **ME**, my marriage, my life.

I didn't exist in this life anymore. I walked around the house in the middle of the night not knowing what to do with myself. I was annoyed at my own breathing. I turned the TV on to drown out my breathing but then turn it off when the show started any feelings. In my nothingness, it was unbearable to feel anything. *How could I feel anything if I didn't exist?* I sat in darkness trying not to cry or breathe or be at all.

He didn't come when I was crying and screaming uncontrollably, which was proof that I wasn't really there. I would get up before the world was awake, drive to the park, and scream until I couldn't scream anymore. I was so broken that I thought something in me would physically break, and I would wake up in a hospital.

One evening, I was crying under the covers in my bed. He came in to tell me to stop crying, crying wasn't going to fix anything. I begged him to fix it. I told him what to say and what to do. He said he wasn't going to do any of that. He looked at me with pity and worry and asked, "Are you going to be okay? What are you going to do?"

Lightning went through my body. The girl inside woke up!

"What am I going to do?! I'm going to keep being a mother. I'm going to keep gardening and canning salsa. I'm going to have friends and hobbies. I'm going to have the best damn life you've ever seen! Nothing has changed except for you. You just won't be there. But me... I am still here, and I am still living this life. And I will make it great!"

*There she is... geesh!* Thank goodness she was still in there. I had just about drowned her out.

## The World is Not Happening To You

In Victor Frankl's book, *Man's Search for Meaning*, he has everything taken from him in a concentration camp, his titles, his job, his family, his clothes, his hair, all his possessions, even his dignity. Everything we have that we believe defines us, he was stripped of. His education was disregarded, his role as a father, husband, brother, even a *human being* were all destroyed and taken away. They literally tried to make him and his people non-existent. He was just a number.

Victor resolves that the experience held no purpose. He discovers that *he* holds purpose for the experience. He sees beauty in the sunsets. He creates friendships. He inspires hope in strangers. He uncovers the ability to happen to this meaningless, dark, horrid place.

Here was a man who was in a concentration camp experiencing pain we will never know, and he was asking himself how he exists in this horrific circumstance. He had an entire regime working to make him disappear. And yet, he was asking himself how do I show up here?

This concept made me rethink every negative experience I had ever had. I replayed them with this idea. *What if experiences weren't happening to me, but rather, I was meant to happen to them? What if I was made to show up for each experience?*

Bad weather always feels like it's something that happens to us. We are so inconvenienced by a rainy day. *So, how could I show up for a rainy day?* I would make it a cozy, inside day, pop popcorn and watch movies. Maybe, put on our rainboots and go stomp in the puddles. Maybe, lay on my bed and listen to the rain. Or we could pass out ponchos to the homeless. This is how I can *happen* to a rainy day rather than have it happen *to me.*

Laundry also seems to happen to me continually. *How can I happen to the laundry?* I could play my favorite music, or watch a show, and listen to that podcast. I could open the windows, burn a candle, and take deep breaths. I can dump the piles on my kid's bed and walk away. Laundry, the rain, an affair, even a concentration camp does NOT have to happen *to you.*

How do you happen to today?

## Bringing Happy to the Happiest Place on Earth

Excruciating back pain had not been alleviated after several trips to the chiropractor. I had broken my tailbone when I slipped on the stairs. The pain caused me to sit to the side. Sitting to the side caused my hips to get out of place, which caused even more pain. We were about to leave for Christmas at Disneyland, and my back was the worst it had ever been. I didn't know how I would even make it in the car to the airport. Never mind the flight and the rides. But we were going, and I was going to figure it out.

Tears streamed down my face in the middle of the flight. The pain was overwhelming. I felt like I was going to break in half when it was time to stand up. The flight attendant gave me an ice pack, and I drowned out the pain with hyper focus on a movie.

We got to the hotel, and I did all the stretches I had been trained to do. I iced it and took the maximum dose of Ibuprofen and Tylenol. The next morning, still in excruciating pain, I was angry and resentful. Because of my practice to self-awareness, I recognized that my feelings were getting in the way of my availability to the experience. So, I did the work to get the pain out of the way. I took a few minutes to read some inspiration. I took a moment of meditation. I reached out to a friend who provides clarity and guidance. The pain would still exist, but it would not be happening to me. After creating a peace within myself, it was time to ask, *How can I be useful?*

A random thought came. I had tiny little *Would you rather?* game cards in my purse. I could get those out while in line and make waiting in line a more pleasant experience. Weird thought... *How would that help my back?* But I wasn't going to argue with it. So, I made sure to bring the little cards, and I resolved to look for opportunities to be useful at Disneyland.

Standing in line for the tea cups, everyone around me was annoyed and bothered at how long the wait was. Little kids were nagging, and parents were already tapped out of patience. I remembered my card game idea. I took them out and started asking my family would you rather questions, and guess what happened?! The little boy next to us in line started playing along, and then his mom, and then the family on the other side of the rope. We all started laughing and discussing if you'd rather have a dragon as small as a kitten or a kitten as big as a dragon. It was so much more fun than just standing there.

After the ride, we took a potty break. There was a man pushing his wife into the restroom in her wheelchair. He got to the door and let her go while she argued, "You have to take me the rest of the way in!" He replied with outright refusal. I offered, "I can take you in if that's okay?" She agreed.

As we made our way to an available stall, I learned that she was local and came to Disneyland often. She had horrible back problems and pain through her feet. I asked how she can enjoy it in so much pain. She simply said, "Oh, I just love it here."

I don't know when I realized that I wasn't experiencing any pain. I'm not sure if it was still there and I was just focused on other things, but I enjoyed riding all the rides that day. When we got back to the hotel room, I didn't even think to get an ice pack. I enjoyed the rest of our vacation without pain.

When I am in pain, when people don't like me, when my car breaks down, when I have a bad hair day, when people make bad choices, when the weather isn't my way, when anything and everything just happens, it's no longer happening to me. I am here to happen to the world. I would've never found the girl inside without the pain of being broken open.

It is the pain that has led me to myself. It has made me cling to Her. The **ME** that can't be destroyed. The **ME** that not even death can take away. Breaking is required to see what's inside. When you know you are not your body, your titles, your relationships, then you will know Her. The girl inside, **SHE** cannot be destroyed, not ever.

# WAKE HER UP

# CHAPTER 7

# GET OUT OF BED

*Grant me the serenity to*
*accept the things I cannot change,*
*The courage to change the things I can,*
*and the wisdom to know the difference.*
*Serenity Prayer*

After my first baby, I noticed something in my chest would pop and click when I did sit ups. It didn't hurt, it was just troubling. The doctor said that I had a broken xyphoid process; that little triangular piece of cartilage that rests in the middle of your rib cage in front of your heart. He said it was common, and there was nothing he could do about it. It should get better over time.

It got worse. It was hard to breathe if I slept on my right side. It felt like my chest was collapsing or pinching if I lay on my stomach. I asked a few doctors over the years, but everyone said there was nothing they could do. I found a chiropractor that could adjust it, which was terrifying, but it helped for a few weeks before it slid back out of place. Fifteen years passed believing that there was nothing I could do.

I started doing yoga and slowly started noticing that my xyphoid process was feeling more swollen. It was getting more and more painful. I was hesitant to hug people and have my daughter jump in my arms. Finally, one night while trying to do yoga and laying flat on my stomach, I thought to myself...

*This is crazy, no way can I live like this the rest of my life, surely there is something I can do.*

My husband said, "Maybe you can get it removed," and Googled it. There it was, several stories of people having it successfully removed, saying that it was a simple surgery with little to no risk. The next day, I called an orthopedic surgeon in the neighborhood, and he was able to get me a referral to a cardiovascular surgeon.

Only a few days later, I was in his office. He looked at it for five minutes and said, "Yeah, that's bad. Let's take it out. When would you like to do it?" Jokingly, I said, "Tomorrow." Knowing that it could just be gone, "Get it out right now!" He said, "How's 5 am?"

"Seriously!? Yes!"

I went down for a CT scan and was back being prepped for surgery the next morning.

When the doctor came in to show me my CT scan, he said, "You ready for this!?" He showed me the picture of my xyphoid process. It looked like a crooked two-pronged fork in the middle of my chest. He pointed out where it was broken in eight places. He said that a normal xyphoid process is 1 centimeter long and mine was 3.5. He said, "Yeah, we need to get this out. I can't believe you've lived with it this long."

In less than a 20-minute surgery, it was out. When I woke up, air rushed into my lungs. It felt like too much air. Imagine standing in front of a jet engine trying to breathe. It was like that. Over the next few days, I would have to get accustomed to more air in my lungs. I had been living with a stick jabbing into my ribs for 15 years!

And the whole time, I could've just cut it out.

Some of us have been lying in bed complaining that there has to be another way. We are sick of this pain, this suffering, this dull existence. While others are saying, that's just the way it is. Endure to the end. If you have enough faith, your bed should be enough. It's just going to take time... as in there won't be any pain in heaven.

But then you see someone living on the outside. You can just **GET OUT OF BED**. You can leave, cut it out, put it down, quit, start, move, change. If the **HER** isn't loud enough yet inside yourself, hear this... **LIFE IS FOR LIVING** not **ENDURING**.

Get out of bed!

## No More Homework

She is stubborn and headstrong, determined and incredibly talented. She has always been a daddy's girl. The divorce was devastating to her. And the devastation never ended for her. Going back and forth was always awful. As she grew into a teenager, there was more fighting. Her dad and I didn't agree on parenting styles, and that caused more confusion.

I was in therapy to know what to do. I was reading the parenting books and trying all I could to live up to my precious title of mother. Until one day, the line was crossed, and she would be living with her dad until things got better.

Weeks turned into months. She was not coming back. I had failed. I had lost her. *How do I be her mother when she's not here?* A mother does laundry, makes dinner, and helps with homework. She is here when you get home from school and drives you to all your activities. She gets you groceries and toilet paper. She reminds you to turn off your light and go to bed. I was doing none of that for her anymore. I was nothing, I was worse than nothing, I had failed her and myself.

Despite all I had experienced, all I had learned about titles not mattering, and what people think of me not being my business, it all seemed to be useless. I again found myself feeling like nothing. I was an unwanted nothing, a failure again.

This darkness was familiar and terrifying. It had taken so much pain and effort to pull myself from this darkness before. Something went off inside of me that refused to keep doing this every time someone else decided I wasn't what they wanted. Or rather, when other people weren't what I expected them to be.

I prayed and prayed for direction. I prayed to know how to be her mother. I prayed that all my thoughts of what a mother should look like would be taken so I could see something else. I felt directed to do nothing. *(Worst answer ever!)* I just wanted to fix it! I was willing to do anything because what I was trying wasn't working. I stayed away for a while. No texts, no calls, no notes, no treats, no money. And after a few weeks, things seemed to get even worse!

I went back to God very angry. "You said to do nothing, and you would fix this!" What came to my mind next altered my understanding of myself forever. "I have been a perfect Father to her, and she can still not accept my help. You, Marcella, are exactly the mother for her. You are doing it well, and she can still choose to not want it."

And just like that, I **FINALLY** understood that I am enough as I am. All my good and my bad. My imperfections and my half-efforts are all as they were created to be, and **SO WAS SHE.**

Several months went by with very little interaction. I was working on myself and trying to understand my part in our relationship. I realized that my idea of how she was going to be happy was what had caused so much pain and resentment. I had decided what our relationship was going to look like, and anything else was a failure on both our parts. I had decided what a good girl looked like, talked like, acted like, who her friends were, and how she interacted with the world. Anything else meant I had failed or she was doing it wrong.

My idea of her happiness was the cause of so much contention, judgment, and ultimately a conditional type of love. *Who was I to say that her journey wasn't creating the exact experiences she needed to grow and learn in her own way? Who was I to decide what the correct way to happiness was for her?*

I had to let go of everything I thought our relationship would or should be. I had to let go of the way I thought she would or should be. If it was true that I was enough with all of my short comings and attempts at trying, then so was she. We were both worthy of loving as we are.

We met for lunch. And for the first time, I sat across from my beautiful daughter and saw her. I had nothing to fix or correct. I was so incredibly grateful that I was at lunch with her. I didn't care at all what she wore, how her makeup was or how she talked about her friends. All of it was wonderful because she was there. And for the first time, I loved her unconditionally.

I knew I was a whole person no matter her choices. And so was she. I was a safe place for her. She was no longer judged or picked apart. She was appreciated, loved, and adored. She didn't have to fix anything or change anything. Anger could happen, and I could walk away whole. I knew how to remove myself without feeling responsible. I was aware when I was responding with love versus fear and needing things my way.

I told her that I was sorry that I had allowed my idea of her happiness to get in the way of our relationship. I said that I would try to respect her journey and be available when she needed me. I was expecting her to slam the door and walk away. She took a long pause, then just looked at me and said thank you.

We hugged a real hug, and I knew that while I would never get the motherhood experience that I had longed for, I would get something I never imagined and omething I had never seen before. From me letting go of my way, I found unconditional love for her and myself.

She is exactly as she is, and I am exactly me, and people get to choose whatever they want. That's one of the greatest parts about being human.

I could've been the perfect employee, the perfect wife, the perfect mother, and people can just decide that they don't want that. There is no need to convince, explain, push, or prove them otherwise. There is just me, being me, trying to let go of what is in my way of being me.

## She was in the Cake

Getting out of a bed filled with resentment and anger seems an obvious necessity to finding myself. Letting go of concepts that I had built my entire faith upon felt terrifying and reckless, but I was being introduced to a peace and connection that I had never known. This sparked curiosity about my faith, and I dared to let go of what I knew about God and everything I thought I knew about myself.

I was raised in the Mormon religion. I went to church every Sunday and sang songs about Heavenly Father. I learned that I was a child of God. I learned how to pray to Heavenly Father, and that I was made in the image of Him. At almost 40 years of age, I had never even thought to ask if I had a Heavenly Mother. I was always told she was too sacred to talk about. Then, my younger sister shared a poem with me called, A *Motherless House* by Carol Lynn Pearson. The words pierced my soul.

*...I yearn for the day*

*Someone will look at me and say,*

*"You certainly do look like your Mother."*

~Carol Lynn Pearson

I cherished my relationship with God and didn't want to offend Him. Yet, my heart and mind had been opened to the possibility of a Heavenly Mother. I had to find her. I was willing to let go of everything I had been told to seek my own truth.

Late one night, my son reminded me that he wanted to make a cake for his book report that was due the next day. It was already 10 p.m. He offered to stay up late and do whatever he could to help. I knew that the best place for him would be to go to bed and be rested for the next day. I had taken a cake-making class with the talented *Cake by Courtney* a few weeks prior and was excited to put these new skills to the test. I turned on a movie and got to work. I had never made a cake from scratch and certainly not a layer cake. I followed the recipe step-by-step. I mixed it for the exact minutes on the recipe. I baked it, I let it cool the precise amount of time, then I wrapped it and put it in the freezer.

The next morning, my son helped frost the cake. He chose where to put the sprinkles and what to add on top. It was the most amazing cake I had ever made. We drove to school and before he got out of the car, he looked at me and said, "Mom, this is amazing! You're wonderful, thank you." I watched him beam as he carried his cake into school.

I was overjoyed that his idea had become a reality. Because of his idea, I was able to use the skills I had to help him. And then, sitting in the school drop-off zone, I found Her, my Mother. This is how my Mother works. She can't wait for me to think up wonderful things so she can use her abilities to help them become reality. She exists.

Over the last few years, I have continued to develop a relationship with Her by learning how to speak to Her and hear Her. I have dared to ask things that challenge what I have always been taught and seek my own truths. I see Her now, just as you would see both your Father and your Mother in your daily life.

My brother lost his keys and had told us how he had looked everywhere for several days, until one day he took his dog for a walk and there in the trees, someone had hung his keys in order to be found. He shared this on our families' group text, and he said that Heavenly Father had answered his prayers. I replied in text saying, "I don't think so. That seems more like a Heavenly Mother thing."

I could imagine God saying, "This will be a good lesson for him to learn. He will have more appreciation for things and maybe he'll be less careless next time." And Heavenly Mother saying, "Oh, but watch the look on his face when he sees them hanging on the tree today. Let's do that!"

I don't write any of this to preach to you or to tell you what is truth and what isn't. I only write my experience to shake you up a bit. Maybe this is really out there and uncomfortable for you. Hopefully, it's uncomfortable enough for you to ask yourself why you believe what you believe. Is there more? What are you hanging onto that might be in the way of more truth and understanding?

There is no book that told me how to develop a relationship with a Heavenly Mother. No one told me what She looks like or how She talks to me. Just because I wasn't taught those things, doesn't mean She doesn't exist. Letting go of my understanding of God has allowed me to have a new and more expansive understanding of my myself, the world and other's beliefs well beyond my imagination.

I have developed a great yearning to know for myself what is truth. I want to know it straight from the source without human fears, resentments, judgments, ideas, or self-seeking. *If no one ever told me there was a God, would God exist?*

If no one ever told you who you are supposed to be, how would you exist?

## No Masks

In February of 2020, Love Woolies was about to celebrate our best month ever. We were about to do $10,000 thanks to our new cashmere scrunchies. I told the team we would go to a spa if we hit the $10 grand goal. Queue the pandemic.

A friend shared with me that the CDC was asking people to make masks and thought since I have a team of seamstresses that we could help. I asked the girls if they would be willing to donate their time. We received donated fabric from neighbors and made a few hundred masks that first week, but we didn't know where to donate them.

Another friend sent me a link to an organization that had put together a database of clinics in desperate need of masks. Now we could see the overwhelming need. Hundreds of thousands of masks were being requested. We spent another week making masks and made 1,500 masks in two weeks.

Our customers started asking if we would sell them. I did not want to sell the masks. They were not our product. They weren't wool. They weren't repurposed. We were still figuring out how to make them consistently and efficiently. We didn't have quality control in place because they needed to be done so quickly, and I didn't have access to new fabric.

They didn't go with our brand at all. Masks next to repurposed wool mittens just seemed silly and far from our brand's image.

I got an email from a customer back East explaining that without a mask, she could not go to the grocery store and she had no idea where to get a mask. She begged me to send her a mask.

I started realizing what level of desperation we were dealing with. I was going to have to let go of my resistance and be useful. It served a bigger purpose to make the masks available. I came up with a plan—for every mask sold, we would donate a mask to a clinic or an essential worker.

We put them on the site. I began thinking. *If our customers can't find the masks anywhere, then others are probably in the same situation.* I put the masks on a Facebook ad so that maybe another lady needing to go to the grocery store could get a mask.

The next morning, I woke up to 50 orders for masks. By the end of the day, we had sold over 1,000 masks, and it wasn't slowing down.

We hired 50 seamstresses over the next two weeks and made 6,000 masks every week for three months. It was just me and my husband filling orders. We would be up until 3 am cutting fabric and creating mask kits for seamstresses. I'd sleep for a few hours and get up to fill orders up to the point that I could race to the post office to drop off a car load of mask orders, Door Dash dinner for the family, and do it all again. It was an entrepreneur's dream come true!

One day, I was putting in the 10th load of fabric into the washing machine and felt so overwhelmed. *What had I done? How will this ever end? My kids are sad and missing their friends. All my friends are coming up with fun quarantine activities and my kids are being utterly ignored while I run this crazy operation of mask making.*

I thought maybe I had done the wrong thing. *Maybe I should stop now and go back to what Love Woolies actually does.*

I sat in the pile of fabric and cried. I poured my heart out to the heavens asking for direction. I was greeted with the thought of my grandpa saying, "The world needs masks, and you have the ability to make them, stop your crying, get up! We are doing this!" That is exactly what my grandpa would say and do. As a firefighter, he did what it took to save lives.

So, I let go of my worry about the kids. I let go of the way I thought things were supposed to be. *Why would I think I knew what a life during a pandemic was supposed to look like anyway?* I accepted that this was my role during the unknown. I would trust that everything else would be as it should as I did what I needed to do.

Letting go allowed for a flood of things well beyond my imagination. We were featured on several news stations. We provided distraction and purpose to 50 seamstresses and over 250 volunteers. We provided masks for over 120,000 people. We were able to donate masks to 10 schools. We provided income for 60 women who had lost portions of their income during the pandemic. I could've easily stopped at the 1,500 we first made and gone back to what we had always done. I chose to let go and get out of the way.

## Star of the Show

I was driving my son to a theater audition. He had only been acting for a year. This audition was at the largest theater in the state, and it was for a starring role. I told him we were going for practice. It would be a fun experience.

He practiced and practiced, but all week, his voice was hoarse and weak. Driving to the audition, he was singing and singing and it was getting worse and worse. His efforts turned to tears and frustration. "Why can't my voice just work? Why do I have to have allergies? This is so dumb. It's going to be so embarrassing!"

Initially, I wanted to say, "Suck it up, stop crying. It's not that big of a deal. We aren't going to even go if you're going to act like this." But gratefully, I didn't. I dug deep into what I had learned about things you can't control. I asked him if there was anything he could do to force his voice to sound the way he wanted. No. He couldn't fix his voice. Then we talked about what he could do.

He could drink water, take cough drops, and stay calm. He could be kind and encouraging to everyone there. He could have positive thoughts and say nice things to himself. He could let go of the frustration of all the things out of his control. We paused and prayed for his frustration to be removed and for him to trust the outcome of the day.

The parents sat in the hallway and the producer cracked the door so we could hear them, which never happens. It was strange. The kids sounded wonderful. I was so nervous waiting for him to just get it over with. Then a kid started singing, and it filled the room. My friend nudged me and said, "Isn't that your son?" I replied, "No." She said, "Yes, yes, it is." My heart jumped out of my chest. Even as I write this, tears fill my eyes knowing that I was witnessing the power of letting go enough to let miracles happen.

He walked out of the room and we looked at each other. I asked him, "What happened in there? What was that!?" In total disbelief, he said his voice opened up and it all just came out. "Mom, that was a miracle!"

A few weeks later, we were notified that he got the part. He went on to have months of wonderful experiences beyond anything we could've ever expected. His participation in that play was life changing for him and all those that watched him do it.

There are miracles right outside the door. They aren't coming in and dragging you out of bed. You have to get up, open the door, and let them in. There is an existence you cannot know until you leave the old one behind.

Maybe today it isn't a drastic event such as ending an abusive relationship or quitting a job. Maybe today it's leaving the bed of negative self-talk.

What can you let go of today? Right now. What bugged you today? What would you be without the thought? How can you perceive it differently than ever before? How can you be useful?

Now, put your feet on the floor and just stand there, out of bed. Feel your feet on the floor. Let your new place of existence simply **BE**.

# WAKE HER UP

# CHAPTER 8

# TURN ON THE LIGHT

*This little light of mine, I'm going to let it shine.*
*This little light of mine, I'm going to let it shine.*
*This little light of mine, I'm going to let it shine.*
*Let it shine, let it shine, let it shine.*
*(A Song I sung in Girl Scouts)*

## Don't Sell the Trumpet

I was in kindergarten when my Dad sold his trumpet. I remember being sad. I still think about that day and have wondered why it made me so sad. Maybe I knew I wouldn't see my Dad being silly with his puffy cheeks anymore. The house wouldn't be filled with a crazy trumpet sound and funny dances. Maybe I knew I was losing a piece of joy in my life because my Dad was giving up his.

My Dad also loved pottery. He had a wheel and a kiln in the garage. The cold, wet clay with the smell of mud is still home to me. My kindergarten class walked to my house for a field trip to watch my Dad do pottery. I found so much joy in what brought my Dad joy.

We moved when I was 6 years old. The kiln and clay didn't come with us. There was no more pottery. He started remodeling our home which seemed to fill his passion to create something new.

He rebuilt cars and remodeled houses. Working with his hands, restoring, and creating things was his joy. He thought of ideas and made them happen. Something broke, and he would fix it. Others would see a rundown gross house, but he saw a beautiful place for a family to call home.

At 12 years old, we moved to Utah. My Dad served in the Air Force and was assigned to teach at the ROTC at Brigham Young University. More creativity and teaching seemed to fuel his soul. He spent evenings on the karaoke machine singing the Carpenters soundtrack over and over. When he wasn't singing, he was finishing the basement or ripping out the orange countertops in the kitchen. When those were done, he bought a purple Corvette to clean up and resell.

Then he was transferred to a desk job, an hour north, at Hill Air Force base. We rented a house, so there was no more remodeling. I don't know where the karaoke machine went. I turned 16, and the old fixer-upper car was replaced by a car I could actually drive. The TV took up the time that would've been spent painting or laying tile. He dove into a deep depression and sunk into the couch for several years.

As I write this, I wish I had been able to see it. I wish I would've bought him a trumpet, or just busted down a wall on purpose just so he would've had to rebuild it.

A few years later, he had been swallowed up in addiction and darkness. In the middle of the nothingness, he walked past a man selling art in front of a grocery store and it sparked curiosity and intrigue. He followed the spark and got to know this man. This led to a business venture that would pull my Dad off the couch and allow him to live again. We all watched as he breathed air back into his life. He was coming back.

He and my mom built the art gallery business for several years. After selling the company, they started another, and then another. He and my mom's relationship grew into something new and wonderful. They moved into a home that brought joy and comfort. He took great pride in landscaping and maintaining a beautiful yard. Many evenings were spent on the back deck soaking in the fresh flowers and enjoying fresh veggies from the garden. The passion for business and creating had always been in him.

His joy, his map, his purpose, had been built in. The more he nourished it, the more it grew. Leaning into his interests and passions cultivated new air and nourishment to everyone around him, just as his garden did.

My parents are now retired and live in Arizona. My Dad plays golf every day and became a real estate agent. One day, my husband said he needed to go look at a car for my Dad. A few hours later, he pulled up and my heart soared out of my chest. Tears filled my eyes. There it was... a gold 1969 Corvette. And I knew, **MY DAD WAS BACK!** The kindergarten field trip Dad... **HE WAS BACK!** This was the guy that played the trumpet. This was the Dad that helped me create a hand-crank generator for a science experiment. The guy that existed before he got swallowed up in jobs, bills and life. The guy that gave me piggy backs and sang at church parties, that guy... **HE WAS BACK!** The world was suddenly brighter.

Now he and my mom are flipping houses again. Creating and restoring is built inside of him. By my Dad pursuing his talents and passions, my Mom is finding that she's a pretty damn good designer and decorator. It's so fun to have them call and have so much to tell us, rather than only asking about the grandkids. They send picture updates, and I get so excited to go out and visit knowing that their lives are full of passion and energy.

Even though he's 12 hours away, just knowing that my Dad exists fully makes the world I live in a brighter place. If his joy existed in him all this time, then my air and my joy exists in me right now. The kind that wakes you up in the morning. The kind of joy that makes you buy a gold 1969 Corvette just because it lights you up.

Your joy is not a pastime. What wakes you up and fills your soul is not a hobby. It is not extra.

*Joy is your air.*
*Without it,*
*you aren't living.*

## Just Dance

I had locked myself in the guest bedroom in protest of my marriage falling apart. I refused to eat or drink, proving that I no longer existed. I cried and begged for him to leave her, while sitting alone in a dark corner of the world.

I was tired of all the lies. I wanted my life back. Trying to decide what bedroom to sleep in every other night was confusing. Not wanting to pass him in the hallway paralyzed me in my house. This had gone on for months. I had lost all hope.

Weeks before finding out about the affair, I had applied to be an assistant coach for the high school dance team. I had forgotten about it during all the devastation. While I laid in the dark, covered in despair, I received an email. I didn't look at it right away. I felt unworthy of any interaction or acknowledgment of my existence.

I finally looked at it. They said they wanted me to start right away.

*No way! How could I possibly take on something new in the middle of my destruction zone?* I was a mess. Probably not the best person to be coaching and motivating high school girls.

Yet, I watched my fingers type a reply, "Great, I'll be there."

Without warning, the lights flipped on and the room flooded with energy. My thoughts were instantly consumed by choreography and song choices. I listened to music and watched different dance styles. There wasn't time or room for all the thoughts that had been destroying me, the thoughts had kept me locked up and tortured. With one simple change to my thoughts, my soul lit up, and the chains fell off.

I hadn't found a way to fix my marriage. He was still having an affair. The guest bedroom was going to keep being my bedroom off and on. I had no idea what was going to happen, but it seemed to not matter anymore. All I knew was I needed to show up to the high school on Thursday at 5 p.m. to dance. Before then, I had to choreograph a warm-up routine. That was all I needed to feel alive.

The next day was filled with loud music. The kids and I danced and danced. I choreographed with my son on my hip, and my daughter learning all the moves. We giggled and forgot that our family was breaking. The pain was pushed out by joy.

Showing up to drill team practice twice a week saved me. There were days that I drove to the high school crying about the heart wrenching new findings of the day. I'd wipe my tears on the way in. I was invisible until I stepped into that gym, and then there I was. I still existed, and I mattered to the girls on that team. We worked hard and made an incredible amount of progress. As much as they might think that they needed me, they saved me and carried me through the darkest moments of my life. Not only did *my* joy and *my* passion help to save me but so did the girls pursuing *their* talent and *their* joy.

I started asking myself, What do *I* like?

How would *I* like to spend my day?

How would *I* like to decorate my room?

Do *I* want to shave my legs?

Do *I* eat breakfast?

Do *I* want to do my hair today?

What would *I* like to have for dinner?

What color pillows do *I* like?

They were simple questions. I didn't realize at the time, but I was finally looking for me inside of me. I would discover that what I needed most was me.

I jumped on the trampoline and played in the fall leaves with my kids in their pajamas. I made homemade pizza. I played songs from my high school years. I got my haircut, bought new clothes, and booked a vacation with a friend.

I stood a little taller and walked a little faster. One night, I was walking out the door to watch the dance team perform. He was still living at the house and said, "Wow, you just seem so good." I replied, "Yeah, I really am so good."

Walking to my car, I thought to myself... *Where have I been for so long? I've been in here the whole time. Sad for him that he failed to notice. But, also sad for me that I never noticed either.*

I kept asking what was in me, and in the middle of my life falling apart and my dream of a happy family crumbling all around me, I was becoming more whole. *How could this be? How could everything around me be falling apart, and I was finding a joy I had never known?*

Dancing had just been a thing I loved back then. It was just for fun... *Or was it?* Now it had become my air. It woke me up and reconnected me to myself and my kids. This thing that I thought was gone, it had been in me the whole time. It was there to save me. *What else was in me?*

## Lights, Camera, Action

My daughter was in a high school play as one of the small children. Instead of my son sitting there waiting for her to be done, he learned the dances and songs. By the third practice, I asked if they could use him, and he was added in. Opening night, I thought my older daughter would light up and own the stage. I thought this would be her *thing* that she would shine and be in full character. To my surprise, there was my son, beaming ear to ear and shining brighter than I had ever seen him. He had done a hip hop class before and loved it, and the recital went well, but this, this was something else entirely. This was seeing all of him, everything he was created to be, all his passion, joy, and talent right there in the lights for everyone to see.

He took summer acting camps. The passion and talent grew quickly. He landed a role in the local Youth Christmas Carol and never got tired of showing up for long hours and doing the show over and over and over. He was cast as Aladdin in the summer camp. To see him be the lead and show up bigger than life at 10 years old seemed to fill the entire house, neighborhood, and his school with boundless light and energy.

I never had to talk him into going to a recital or a show. He missed out on birthday parties, school events, and time with friends and family. He stayed excited every night he came home from a show. He landed the role of Les in the Broadway Newsies at the local community theater. *(My 14-year-old heart was out of her mind!)* It was a paid role, and it was a huge time commitment. I thought he would get tired and burnt out. That never happened, not even when he was actually tired. It didn't matter, the show, lights, singing, dancing, cheering—it all superseded any exhaustion.

I couldn't help but think... *I want that. Whatever he's got, I want that in my life. Does it even exist at my age or in my world?* And, of course, I was thinking this while doing dishes and waiting for him to call so I could get back in the car for the fourth time that day to pick him up. I wanted to find that spark and thrill in me. If that exists, it's got to exist somewhere in me too. I had to find it.

It had been over 10 years since coaching the dance team, and I already knew that dance was the thing that lit me up. *But I'm 40 years old now. Where would I even begin?*

I had the idea to find an adult class and give that a try. It was merely just a thought while I was blow drying my hair. An hour later, my friend sent me a text asking if I would want to take a dance class with her. Punch passes were half off, and she was going right then to the studio to get one. I literally started typing that I had things to do as I was standing in a house with everyone off at school and my husband at work. *Why, why would I say I couldn't go?* I erased what I typed and said, "Yes!!!"

We went to the studio and bought the passes. I had two weeks to worry about what I was going to wear and who else would be there. *What if I felt like a dork and it wasn't the fun that I thought it would be?*

The day finally came, and we were both so excited. We showed up to the class and it was a Jazz class. The instructor taught us technique, which I always hated. He was asking a 40-year-old mother of four who hasn't been in a dance studio for 20 years to do a double pirouette and leaps. Hilarious. It was nice to be in a dance studio and just move my body, but it was not thrilling or energizing. It was uncomfortable and awkward. It was not what we thought it would be. Two weeks went on like that until we realized we had been going to the wrong class.

When we finally got to the right class, shazam! There it was! All the thrill with the soul- awakening movement to the beat. The movement of the universe when you are in unison with five other souls creating one whole energy. I certainly didn't have the moves I used to, but it didn't seem to matter. Dancing still felt like flying.

## Discomfort - Required

If you wanted to take a painting class, you'd have to enroll in the class, arrange your schedule, and sacrifice time in other areas. You may even worry about who else is going to be there. Are you going to be the worst one? What if you can't do it? You will have to drive there and actually get out of your car and walk into a room of strangers. You will have to sit in front of a canvas not knowing what to do.

And *then* the learning begins.

The first class is boring. It's awkward and informative. You don't even paint at first, but you go back the next week and take a chance at getting to know the person next to you. Finally, you pick up your brush. It's time to put paint on the canvas. It's scary and uncomfortable. What if you mess it up? What if you can't fix it? What if you're horrible? What if this was a waste of time and money? Your canvas has paint on it, but it doesn't look like anything yet.

You make yourself show up again. This time, you connect a little deeper with your new friend and your canvas has some-thing on it that resembles fruit. Several weeks go by, you can't wait to go, you and your new friend are going out for dinner after class. You're looking forward to learning the next skill because now you know you can learn new things. And you're not half bad. Who knew you could paint? Who knew you would love it?

**YOU DID.** No wonder you signed up for the class. The girl inside wanted to paint.

The doors of discomfort need to be relabeled as

*Doors to:*
### *EVERYTHING YOU EVER WANTED AND MORE*

## Fight for the Triple Lutz

Sometimes finding our talent and our joy comes with a fight. My oldest daughter decided several years ago that she wanted to be a figure skater. She had been to the ice rink for a few months practicing the little she had picked up from others. She could already do more tricks than most of the general public. For Christmas, all she wanted were her very own pair of ice skates and lessons. She counted down the days to her lessons believing that she would be able to skip all the primary classes and go straight to the next level. The lesson didn't go as expected. She came home beaten down and disenchanted. She was told that she needed to go down a level. I thought that would be that. She would never go back. We had wasted our money and would be left with an angry, defeated little girl.

To my surprise, she fearlessly went back to face the disappointment. She was willing to do whatever it took to pursue what was in her. Her journey has been a continual battle to show up when she was sore and bruised. Many days came with an internal struggle against herself. She fought to get herself there, to get up after a hard fall and do it again. Some days, her mind won, and she didn't get there. There were weeks at a time when she lost the battle and didn't make it to the rink. And yet, she still made progress. There was no ignoring this unexplainable desire to skate.

A few years ago, she started winning the battle daily. She went from a practice a week to five hours a day. We shortened her school schedule to make time for skating. More coaching, more training, additional coaches, and workshops. She is now competing at a level beyond her coach's expectations. Working at the rink and teaching classes, the ice rink is her home. It's where she has found herself.

All of this has come during 7th-12th grade, when we all tend to lose ourselves and are flailing around trying to figure out who we are. This journey came at a point where Kenna did not want to be around me. Yet, for a time, she was okay to have me take her to skating. The look on her face when she is on the ice, the breeze in her hair, the way she holds herself knowing she can skate the way she had once only imagined is priceless. She gets to block the world out as she skates. She gets to feel her ability and determination as she skates and overcomes the falls. She gets to feel joy even when she's bruised, frustrated, and tired. As her mother, I get to see this amazing woman find a piece of who she is. I get the privilege of sharing in her joy. To watch her do something I cannot do and have no desire to do, it's amazing that she does and does it so well. Her fight to pursue her joy has allowed a way for me to show my support and encouragement.

It has saved her on the worst of days. It has provided her a sense of identity in a time where most people don't have one.

You Being *You* is not selfish.

You Being *You* is the greatest service you can give.

What will the world be when more people lean into *their* joy?

How will the world be when more people know who *they* are?

What brings *you* joy?

What has lit *you* up in the past?

What are *you* willing to try?

If you like playing the piano, but it's been several months, play the piano. If you enjoy baking, bake a bit more this month. If you love singing, crocheting, gardening, visiting friends, golfing, hiking, reading... do those things a little bit more. Start asking, watching, and listening.

When you are ready to light up the world, the world will show you the light switch.

# CHAPTER 9

# BRUSH YOUR TEETH

*Have you ever tried to do anything while brushing your teeth? It's impossible. And if you do, you end up holding the toothbrush in your mouth way too long. Then you still have to stand there and finish brushing without doing anything else. It's hard to do nothing. Doing nothing. Being still. Getting quiet. Turning off the thoughts. That is when you will meet HER.*

*Hello, I am You*

Have you ever had one minute of not thinking? Sleeping doesn't count. I read a book that recommended meditating every morning. *What did that even mean? Was I supposed to sit in a yoga pose with my hands in prayer? Were there special candles? Is there a meditation poem or prayer to memorize?* I had no idea.

*And even then, aren't there more productive things I could be doing with my time? Sitting and not thinking... how was that helpful to anyone?*

A friend recommended the book, *Surrender Experiment*, by Michael Singer. He explains how he was annoyed and curious about all the chatter in his mind and his journey to quiet that voice. Through the practice of turning off his thoughts, he seemed to attract everything he needed. His journey was different than anything I'd read in so many other self-help or business books. He was doing less, thinking less, stressing less, and a beautiful successful life showed up.

He piqued my curiosity, and I decided to try quieting my mind. I went to yoga to learn meditation from the professionals. It was quiet, dark, and hot. At first, my mind would race through all the to-dos of the day. I would be in warrior position and creating a new marketing campaign for mittens. Then, in tree pose, I would be sorting through the meal plan for the week.

The instructor tried to guide the classes thoughts. She said, "If you have found your mind wandering off, don't reprimand yourself, simply come back. There is no work to be done here. But also, trust your thoughts. You cannot do this wrong."

The invitation was offered to find inner stillness. I kept going, and I was annoyed by my constant conversation and chatter. It seemed that meditation just wasn't going to be my thing.

She said, "Focus on your breath so much that you can't hear any other thoughts." No matter how loud I breathed, my thoughts just got louder. One morning, during the same struggle to quiet my thoughts, she said, "Say in your mind, I am breathing in, I am breathing out. Keep repeating this while you enjoy the other thoughts becoming quiet."

And for the first time, my thoughts got really, really quiet. It was just me, my breath, my soul, my body, and my mat. In the middle of the day, I was just existing. Doing nothing but breathing and being. *Was this it? Was I meditating?* It felt good. Good enough to want to keep practicing.

I read *The Miracle Morning* by Hal Elrod. He talked about meditating during your morning practice. I had only found mediation on a yoga mat in a studio where there was no distraction of work, home and family. *Where would I find it at home?*

I started waking up early to practice doing and thinking nothing. It felt backwards from going to the gym and working hard. It didn't make sense that life could get better by doing nothing. Yet, I kept hearing the power of meditation in everything I read and listened to. I had to give it a try.

I went to the basement, sat on a little kid's chair, wrapped myself up in a blanket, closed my eyes, and sat there arguing with my own thoughts. Shushing myself every time I started creating lists or marketing plans. I would say *thank you, come back later*, and then get annoyed that I was even thinking about what I was thinking about. The 5-minute timer would ding, and I hadn't found my inner stillness.

I tried again and again. It slowly got better. My thoughts became quieter. One morning, the thought entered my mind that I am not my body and I am not even my thoughts. I am my soul. I gave Her a name. I called myself by my soul's name and said over and over I am Her. I am Her. I had found me.

## YOU ARE NOT YOUR THOUGHTS!

In the middle of my messy unfinished basement, wearing oversized sweats, sitting in a tiny chair surrounded by toys, **I FOUND MYSELF.**

Thoughts continued to evolve about Her. *How can Marcella serve Her better? How can I protect Her? What is it that She has come to accomplish?* And by asking my true self what She needed from me, I would have to get really quiet to listen. She doesn't speak in words; She speaks in stillness. I can't explain It. You simply have to experience it. You exist in the stillness.

Try being still. It may be the one thing you haven't tried. Being still has become the most productive thing I can do.

So, when you are stuck standing in the mirror brushing your teeth, close your eyes. Notice your thoughts swirling around you. Feel the breath coming in and out. Say to yourself, "I am breathing in, I am breathing out." Keep doing this until the thoughts quiet, and you are left seeing HER. Underneath all the thoughts, **THERE YOU ARE.**

## Resting is Productive

Usually, I could run into the chiropractor every other month, and with a pop and a twist, I was good to go. Since dancing in college, my hips would slowly get out of place. It was a regular thing a few times a year to tweak my back. I had gone twice in a week, and by the time I got out of my car from the office, my pain was back. It wasn't staying.

The pain became so severe, I thought I would wake up paralyzed. While driving, I cried from the pain. It hurt to sit, and it hurt to sleep. I would just stand around, rarely sitting, and then overdose on melatonin, ibuprofen, and Tylenol.

I had never considered that my uterus could be causing back pain until a friend said my pain sounded similar to her experience. I made a gyno appointment, and sure enough, I had a prolapsed uterus. My gynecologist recommended a hysterectomy. It couldn't happen fast enough!

Three weeks after I had my xyphoid process taken out, I was back in surgery for a hysterectomy. I was hopeful that recovery wouldn't be too long. A week or two resting sounded wonderful. My Mom made plans to come out and take care of the family so I could recover. The first week, I was in bed all day everyday as expected. The next week, I would get up mid-morning and be with the kids, and get a few things done. By 3 o'clock, I would be back in bed. By the third week, it was getting old and boring.

It seemed the world was totally fine with me lying in bed not participating.

I started to have negative thoughts. *Why did I believe I mattered so much? Obviously, I don't.* I recognized my thoughts going in the wrong direction and started applying the things I had learned. Pause, breathe, know I am not my thoughts. What is real? How can I be useful?

I laid there until my mind became quiet and there was clarity and stillness. Ideas came. I could invite my daughter to bring her dolls into my room. We played dolls on my bed. She set up an entire Barbie world on my windowsill. We played games and watched movies all snuggled in bed.

One day, my oldest daughter came by to tell me about her day. She got in bed with me. My son joined in, and then my youngest. I listened to her stories and watched her figure skating videos. I was all there. All of me. I wasn't doing or thinking of anything else. I was more present than I had ever been.

Looking back at a picture with all of us in bed makes me miss those weeks of stillness and presence. Being still was useful. Literally lying in bed, I was able to be loving, be caring, be creative, be aware, be attentive, be *all* of me. I was **BEING** rather than doing.

## Charlotte

I was reading *Charlotte's Web* to my youngest daughter. Charlotte tells Wilbur the pig that she is going to save his life. He asks her how, and she says she doesn't know yet, but she will. He asks, how will she know? She explains that she will hang upside down and wait for the answer. The answer always comes. She hangs there. Wilbur keeps asking if she knows yet. She says no, but it will come. He keeps asking, and she tells him to eat well and go to bed. She continues hanging and waiting.

Then, she has a thought. If she is clever enough to trick bugs with her web, then she is clever enough to trick humans with her web as well. And she gets to work and saves Wilbur's life. The answer was in her.

*When you can't DO anything, you can simply BE something. Be Still.*

Even if you are sick and being cared for, you are being useful to someone. You are bringing purpose and meaning to the person who is caring for you. When you are not doing things that you believe define you, you will find that **YOU** still exist. You are you, always. She exists in you no matter your physical state. No matter your emotional state. You are Her and She is **YOU**.

Be still long enough to know Her.

Being still is productive.

Scrap your To-Do list and **BE**.

Everything that is to **BE** accomplished today will **BE**.

There is no doing, just **BEING**.

Be the boss.

Be the answer.

Be the kindness.

Be the listening.

Be the love.

Be the fun.

Be the organized.

Be the excitement.

Be the support.

Be the direction.

Be the peace.

Be the happy.

Be the understanding.

Be the protection.

Be the safety.

Be.

## Lost & Found

She was three years old. We went to Kohl's. The past few weeks we had been playing hide and seek. *(And now anyone reading this knows where this story is headed).* I went around one of the clothing racks and poof, she was gone. I called for her, nothing. I walked around and around. I didn't want to go too far, but since I couldn't find her, I ran in a panic thinking all the worst things possible while finding a clerk. They walked around the area with me several times.

Then, she popped out of one of the clothing carousels. She had just stayed there the entire time. She was so proud of herself. Thought it was so funny. I picked her up and hugged her, through tears, I said, "Peek-a-boo. I found you." What do we tell our kids to do when they get lost? Stay where you are. Stand still. We will come find you.

I found myself laying on a yoga mat in a dark hot room. Up to this point in my life, I thought that the only place I could be closest to my true self and my creators was in a Temple built by my church. In the middle of the pandemic, when everything felt scary and the world felt lost, I found myself. Being still at 5 am on a yoga mat, the world melted away, my thoughts became silent, my body irrelevant to my existence. It was me and the endless universe, no end and no beginning. There She was in a way I had never met her before. In a way I can't describe. You will find Her when you get still enough to be found.

So, when you are feeling lost, you know what to do.

### Be Still, You Will Be Found.

## "YOU WILL BE FOUND" LYRICS
## ~ DEAR EVAN HANSEN

*Even when the dark comes crashing through*

*When you need a friend to carry you*

*When you're broken on the ground*

*You will be found*

*So let the sun come streaming in*

*'Cause you'll reach up and you'll rise again*

*If you only look around*

*You will be found*

## Refrigerator Moment

I was hustling around the kitchen trying to get dinner ready for everyone. My son kept asking me to help him with his homework. I was frazzled and annoyed. No one was helping, and everyone was asking for things... even the dog was barking! I recognized that I was about to transition from making dinner to helping with homework. I opened the fridge to put things away. Before closing the door, I paused, took a breath, and asked myself, *How do you show up to helping with homework? Answer: Calm, understanding, and encouraging.* I took a deep breath and closed the door.

I walked to the table, sat down, and all the frazzle was gone. Dog still barking, kitchen still messy, and still, no one was pitching in. But I was calm, encouraging, and understanding while helping with homework.

## *A Big Move*

Love Woolies had been in my basement for five years. With all the mask making in addition to the wool production, we were not going to fit for the next season. I had six girls coming in and out of the house on a daily basis. During breakfast, my manager would walk in the door, sometimes join us for pancakes and go upstairs to work. An hour later, my production manager would come on in, say hello to the dogs and head to the basement.

One day, I opened the door to find several bales of sweaters blocking my door and the front room was already filled with more bales of sweaters. I realized that the business has spilled out of my house. We had to move.

I didn't know the first thing about finding a warehouse, but I knew that if we were supposed to be in a warehouse, things would start showing up. I didn't need to stress over it. I needed to BE aware and available to opportunities. Soon after, I met a girl who invited me to a pop-up shop at her space. Randomly she mentioned, "If you are ever looking for a space, it would be great to have you." A week later, a customer called about an exchange, and we got to talking. She just happened to be looking for a new tenant for a warehouse she owned. I knew this was confirmation that it truly was time to move.

I called my friend and we had a deal. I still didn't know how I was going to move everything out, but I didn't stress. I made a few calls, and before I knew it, I had an army of women and their mini vans carrying bins out of my basement.

We had to build a wall in the warehouse. How do you get a wall built? You stay clear of fear and doubt. You have random conversations with people and then all of a sudden there is someone building a wall. No stress required. Just BEING available to everything, anyone, showing up to make it happen.

# Rent

We were in that warehouse for about a year until my friend needed her space back. We moved again. I called a commercial agent to show me a few places. After looking at five different places, the biggest one that was out of our budget felt like the right place. *How could it be the right place?* I didn't have the money for the deposit. It was much more space than we required. But the feeling of home was very clear. It didn't make sense, but I knew it was where we needed to be.

I stayed calm. I took extra time in stillness. I spoke to the universe and said, "This feels like the place for us. We need the deposit," and I went to bed.

The next morning, I received an odd text from a customer. It was a picture of Bernie Sanders wearing sweater mittens. She asked if they were my mittens. I googled Bernie Sanders and the internet was filled with pictures of sweater mittens. A little more digging, and I found that Jen Ellis had made his mittens. She didn't have a website and wasn't selling mittens.

I quickly directed my online ads to show to Bernie Sanders searches. Immediately, we had mitten sales. Overnight, we had made our deposit. Over the next 10 days we would sell more mittens than we did the entire past year.

We moved to the big warehouse a few weeks later.

Despite feeling the need to be there, making rent every month was not easy. I got caught up in the stress and fear of making rent every month. The first few months, I did whatever it took and made it happen. But it cost me being unavailable to my family and myself. I was freaking out the last 10 days of every month.

I finally remembered that I no longer function this way. I trust. I pause. I breathe. I listen. The end of the month was coming again, and making the rent appeared impossible. I chose to not be scared. Not to be frantic. I chose to trust that it was going to show up or I would be able to have a conversation with the owner, or we would need to move. I would trust all of it. Whatever came, it was going to be exactly right for me.

A few days later, I got a phone call asking about our extra space for rent. This guy was asking about a short-term lease for the warehouse. The warehouse was not listed, but he thought he'd call and take a chance that maybe we had some warehouse house space available. They had been planning on moving into a space that same day and things fell through. They needed something right away. His team came over within 30 minutes. By the end of the day, we had a short-term agreement that came with a deposit that covered our rent!

It wasn't necessarily doing nothing because we had to move our entire production department to the other side of the warehouse. Yet, inside, I was calm and still. I could move the entire production department while having stillness.

Stillness is something I have to practice every day. I must commit to it every morning and review it every night. It has helped me in the smallest and biggest of experiences. It takes practice and training. Yes, even doing nothing takes intentional action. Quieting the chaos inside you will become your most powerful skill. It is the key to unlocking **HER**.

# CHAPTER 10

# PUT YOUR PANTS ON

*"But, mom... I can't find my pants!" Jane yells as she's getting ready for school. I yell back, "You have plenty of pants in your drawer. Put something on, let's go!" She fires back, "But I don't like any of those. I just want my Tie Dye ones." I yell back, "Those are dirty and in the laundry. You're going to have to pick something else!" "Ugh!" she grunts. Then stomps. Silence. A few minutes later, she comes down for breakfast in some pants.*

*Her subpar choice of pants allowed her to go to school that day. She got to meet new friends, learn new things, laugh, and help others. She didn't have the exact pants she wanted, but she was able to choose how she showed up in the pants she had. It's time. It's probably been time for a while now. You know it. Stop yelling about how your body isn't right, you don't have the money you need, your house, your kids, your marriage isn't this or that. You want the "Tie Dye pants."*

*JUST PICK SOMETHING! Put them on, and let's go!*

The B Word Book

Making dinners he liked was my way of being selfless. Apologizing and letting him win the argument was me being a loving wife. I gave of myself. I compromised my opinions, my likes and dislikes. I gave up my resistance and vibrance for life. I thought this was what it took to have a happy marriage.

It had been less than a year into my second marriage. Arguments, conversations, and feelings were starting to feel the same as my previous failed marriage. I didn't understand. I had married a completely different human. I lived a totally different life, and yet, there I was experiencing the same relationship.

The frustrations and problems spilled out over messenger to my co-worker all day long. She kept recommending that I read a book called, *Why Men Love Bitches* by Sherry Argov. I immediately said, "No way, a girl like me does not read a book with the word bitches on the cover. And I don't want to be a bitch, so why would I read that? Good wives are selfless, sweet, and put their husbands first. We are meek and mild. Good wives are not bitches. Bitches smoke, are rude, and don't have friends. The boys that like them are like puppies, not men. So, no thank you."

I kept complaining to this co-worker, and she kept giving me great advice. Advice that was working! It wasn't changing him. It was changing me and how I thought, how I talked, how I reacted or didn't react. I became more aware of my emotions. How I thought about his actions and words started to change.

*How did I expect to have a different relationship if I was going to be the same?* I read the bitch book. Of course! I downloaded it on my phone so that I wasn't publicly carrying around the word bitches.

One chapter in, I became aware that I lacked the practice of confidently respecting myself in my marriage. In my efforts to be selfless, I had lost myself and was not an active participant in my marriage. I was getting so caught up in how to make him succeed, I wasn't even playing the game.

If my husband came home grumpy, I would immediately think all of the following:

*Why doesn't he appreciate what I've done?*

*I should've cleaned the house more.*

*I should've worn something different.*

*I should be better at having the kids be more obedient and calm.*

*Doesn't he love me?*

*If I was better, he would be happy.*

Did it ever occur to me that maybe he just had a bad day? Or maybe he was just in a bad mood and it actually had nothing to do with me? **NOPE.**

Did I ever ask myself how I show up for him when he's had a bad day?

How would I be useful to a friend who was grumpy and rude?

How could I be useful to someone that was difficult to be around?

It never occurred to me to ask myself any of this. I was so focused on me being selfless that I wasn't thinking about anyone else.

## Noodles for Dinner

I applied my new *Bitch Mode* over dinner when I decided to make noodles rather than rice. I got home from working a long day at the office. Tage would be home soon after, and we could eat together. I made chicken with sauce and noodles, which sounded good to me. It was ready and hot. I waited a while, and he still wasn't home.

Pre-*Bitch* me would've been super bugged that he wasn't home yet and didn't think to call. I would think he didn't want to eat dinner with me, that I wasn't important, and maybe he was dreading coming home.

New me: I was hungry and chose to eat a warm dinner. I hoped he was okay. I thought how frustrating it must be to have to work late. I turned on a show and started eating. He came home, and I was happy to see him. He said, "Sorry you had to eat alone." Old me would've heard, "Oh, so you started without me, that was inconsiderate." Old me would've stopped eating, let him sit down and change the channel. I would've set my plate down to heat his dinner.

The new me heard, "Sorry you had to eat alone." And I responded with, "Oh no worries, sorry you got stuck at work, dinner's really good, the rest is in the fridge." I said all of this with zero annoyance or underlying hurt. I was happy and whole, with a little sexy sass thrown in.

He stood there for a minute, weirded out that I didn't get up to serve him dinner. I kept my mouth shut and kept looking at the TV, determined to stay in my sexy, sassy *Bitch mode*. He sat down just as I was finishing up, and said, "Oh, did we not have any rice? I think rice would've gone better."

Old me: This would've led to a few days of silence while I simmered on a million thoughts of how he doesn't appreciate me. I had made a nice dinner after a long day, and he had the audacity to suggest rice. At the same time, I would've apologized and been furious, yet gotten up and quickly made some rice.

New me: "Oh, I preferred noodles. But if you want rice, there is some in the pantry you could whip up." He looked at me utterly confused as to why I was being cheerful and yet not getting him some rice. I kept on watching my show as he went to the pantry and got the Minute rice out, and asked how to make it. I told him that the instructions are on the box. He made the rice and burnt it. I cleared my space, and he ate his chicken without any rice. We enjoyed a happy evening together in a marriage that now had two participants.

*How long had I been this way? How long had I allowed myself to think I was in charge of his happiness? When did that become my responsibility, and when did it start overriding my happiness?* Being selfless does not mean to be without your *self*. How can you choose to be self-less if you don't even have your *self* in the first place? I wasn't serving him by not being myself. He married me for me. Not for me to disappear and serve him rice.

I didn't have to change him. I didn't have to have everything the way I thought it should be. He didn't have to talk to me a certain way. He didn't need to appreciate me more. I chose to show up with what I had. Me showing up with what I had made my marriage a better place to **BE**.

During that dinner, I found a spark in me I hadn't seen before. I was not a dinner getter, I was a woman who had just worked a full day who respects herself and her life. My confidence gave him confidence. I provided an emotionally stable partner to come home to. That day, Tage came home to **ALL** of me, and he was in for a ride. *(Come on now, not that kind of ride. Well, maybe more of that since I felt more confident and sexy now).*

A few days after the noodles, Tage and I were having a disagreement, and he was doing that thing where he picks out a word you say and magically turns the argument into something entirely different. The old me would go down that rabbit hole again and again, until I was so turned around that I was apologizing for things I didn't know were an issue. It would end in confusion and guilt. I would walk away not knowing what had happened.

New me: "Um, no, but nice try, that's not what we are talking about." He would try again. "Nope, if you would like to talk about that on another occasion that's fine, but that's not this conversation." He would try again. "Still no, I'm not going down that rabbit hole, try and stay focused on what we are actually discussing." Finally, he said, "Geez, I can't win arguments anymore. Why are you being such a bitch?"

Old me: *Holy crap! Pack my bags. Why don't you love me?*

New me: "I have arrived! I am no longer a doormat. I am an equal part of this relationship. I can stand my ground and respect my full value. There are now two full people in this marriage." I was so proud and thrilled to be the B word. I felt sexy and sassy, bold and strong. I felt loved and respected.

He looked at me with adoration and pride, well, it might have been annoyance, but I saw it as respect. He knew that I wouldn't let him be a jerk. He knew that I would call him out when it wasn't okay. He knew I was going to show up and do my part to contribute to us both being our best selves.

Not sure he knew any of this... but more importantly I **KNEW**. He would not be allowed to be a horrible version of himself because I knew I deserved respect and consideration. He was in a safe place with a strong person that could fight for what was best for herself. Me holding ground for myself held my share of the foundation for our marriage.

I had been the thing that was missing from my marriage. The answer was **ME**.

*If you think something's missing...
it's probably YOU!*

# I Feel Pretty

There were still little pieces of my own insecurities that would creep in. If I was bent over and my crack was showing, he would point it out, try and pull up my pants or pull down my shirt. I thought he was embarrassed by me. I would get uncomfortable and feel bad that my crack isn't nice to look at. Also, I felt guilty that I had dressed poorly equaling an unwelcome view. I would fix my pants and go on, a bit more self-conscious. That is until I watched the movie, *I Feel Pretty*.

I learned once again how to be a *Bitch* about my body. Amy Schumer is standing in a full-length window, bare naked, because she heard the ice cream truck right after sex. Her boyfriend says, "Umm, you know everyone can see you?" Her reply changed my life. She does a sexy shake and sings, **"YOU'RE WELCOME!"**

Now, when my husband points out my crack, I shake my hot ass and sing, "You're welcome!" When he points out that maybe my sweats aren't appropriate to wear to the basketball game, I just say, "You're welcome!" When I show a bit too much cleavage, and he pulls my shirt up because *he* is uncomfortable, I say, "You're welcome!" When I decide to change into the brand-new shirt that I just got at Nordstrom Rack in the car in the parking lot and he says, "People can see you." I again reply with full confidence, "You're welcome!" Thank you, Amy Schumer, for showing me how confidence can look and sound, and how other's discomfort is not my responsibility.

In all those moments, the best part is that I don't get pieces of me chipped away. I exist as all of me, always. I'm not afraid he's going to say something stupid that will offend me and make me crazy for the rest of the day. When he's a jerk, I tell him. When I'm a jerk, he tells me. If he's in a bad mood... he's human, he gets to! It has nothing to do with me.

## It's a Two Player Game

I used to try to make the world around me happy so I could be happy. I used to think that if my kids, my home, and my husband were all happy and peaceful, then I would be happy and peaceful. Making dinner, cleaning house, working out, serving neighbors, cute notes, surprises, laundry, dishes, more laundry, shave my legs, giving and giving. I thought I was all in. I thought I was playing the game and the award at the end was happily ever after.

Imagine you and your partner decide to start playing tennis together. This will be a great opportunity to learn together and have a new experience. You get to the court and decide that it's best if you spend your time cheering him on. Someone needs to make sure he has water and snacks. You sacrifice your playing time to fix his racket, tie his shoes, and take care of his balls. *(I couldn't resist)* Eventually, you start realizing that the game isn't working. You aren't getting better at tennis at all. He's having all the fun, and you've forgotten why you're there.

You aren't playing the game! You aren't on the other side of the net hitting it back. You are so worried about making him uncomfortable or upset. You thought your role was to make sure he could play his best game. In an effort to be selfless, you took yourself out of the game.

We do this with everyone around us... our friends, work, even our kids. We wonder why it's not working. It's because you are on the side lines making sure everyone else has water and snacks. What we all need is you to get in there and play the game.

You, your love, your thoughts, your ideas, your feelings, your laughter, your smile, your presence, your talents, your experiences... **THEY MATTER!** You living your best life is the thing that is missing.

# The Dog Fight

My son and I were driving home when we saw two dogs in the street just a few houses from home. *Were they playing or fighting?* As we drove past, it became very obvious that they were fighting.

A woman I didn't know was sitting on the neighbor's front yard covered in blood and holding her arm. Both dogs were latched onto each other, covered in blood. Another neighbor was keeping the woman's children occupied in a stroller. A man was standing looking at a loss as to how to stop the dog fight.

My husband has a way of being a hero and knowing what to do in emergency situations. We ran in the door and my son yelled, "Dad, two dogs are killing each other. Go help!" My husband ran out the door and down the street. Wondering what I could do to be useful, I grabbed a package of lunch meat and ran towards the dogs.

My husband was able to grab one of the leashes and wrap it around the light pole. The other neighbor pulled the other dog off. Paramedics arrived and started treating the woman who had tried to stop the fight. I didn't know her. I didn't see all that had happened. I thought it best that I didn't get involved and let everyone do their thing.

As I was walking home, I looked back to see the woman surrounded by a group of nearly a dozen men. They had put her on a decorative metal chair in the middle of her driveway. She looked in shock. I said to my son, "It seems she could use a girl over there. But I probably shouldn't get involved." Gratefully, my son said, "Yes, she for sure needs you, Mom. Go."

I walked up and pushed through the group of men surrounding her. Everyone was just standing there looking at her. The paramedic said, "They are just small puncture wounds and there isn't anything more we can do. So, we are going to go. You okay?" She could hardly answer. She was in a daze and shaking. She was clearly not okay. I wrapped my arms tightly around her from behind.

I spoke calmly and clearly, "Breathe, You are safe. Breathe. Breathe with me. You are safe. Your kids are safe. You are okay. Breathe."

I directed my husband to get her water. The paramedics realized that she needed more attention. They stayed longer, waited for her to drink some water and made sure she was breathing more regularly. I moved her into her home to be more comfortable. I wiped the blood off of her arms and legs. I held her while our neighbor, who's a doctor, stitched her puncture wounds. I held her until her husband came home.

Neither I, nor my husband, had any business getting involved, and yet, we were able to provide a solution and comfort. Our experience, our caring, our voices, our understanding, our know-how... it all mattered.

*It's not that you have on the wrong pants. It's how you show up in the pants you have.*

CHAPTER 11

# DON'T SKIP BREAKFAST

*I woke up on the floor, my legs in the bathroom and my body in the hallway. I must've passed out. My two-year-old had gotten up to go potty and needed help getting his pants back on. I remember helping him with his pants. And that was it.*

*I hadn't eaten for several days in protest against my family falling apart. I crawled down the stairs and managed to get a piece of bread. Crawled back up and went to bed.*

*In the morning, I asked my son if he saw Mommy fall down. He said, "I just thought you fell asleep on the floor."*

*I knew I had to feed myself so he wouldn't see his Mom pass out ever again due to her lack of self-care.*

## Stretch Marks

My body wasn't ever something that I had been concerned with. It wasn't something I thought a lot about. I danced in high school and college. My body was always a size that worked for me. I became a personal trainer during college. Having a healthy body happened without much effort, I enjoyed going to the gym. I enjoyed being active. All of that changed while I was pregnant with my first child.

I had gained 70 pounds and topped out at 205. At six months pregnant, I was starting to not like my body. One morning, I stepped out of the shower and was drying off my legs. I felt something odd on the back of my legs. It was like an indent, but it ran all the way down to the back of my knees. It felt like an indentation from sitting on a park bench too long. I looked in the mirror and saw purple tears on the back of both my legs. I had stretch marks! I immediately knew my body would never be the same. It was ruined. I was ruined!!!

I sat on the toilet seat and sobbed uncontrollably not knowing how I would ever feel beautiful again. *How would I ever want to undress in front of my husband? How could I ever wear a bathing suit?* I bought all the magical creams and lotions that claimed to decrease the appearance of stretch marks. Despite my efforts, more showed up, on my hips, on the front of my legs. I thought my stomach had been saved, but after having my baby, my stomach went from tight and round to a deflated balloon with stretch marks all over.

I thought when I had my beautiful baby, they wouldn't matter. My stretch marks, flabby belly, and extra weight would be worth it to have my baby girl.

This is not what I felt. Maybe I didn't love my baby enough? I would tell myself... *Everyone goes through this, you can do it too.* I'd go to the park or the pool and see other moms with newborns and no visible stretch marks, no extra weight. My positive self-talk proved to be lies.

I wish I could say that I did daily affirmations and positive self-talk and accepted the body that I had. That I embraced my stretch marks as scars of honor and love, but that is not what happened. I kept eating uncontrollably and was sad and desperate. I counted on my husband to make me feel important and beautiful, and when he wasn't doing enough, I blamed his lack of effort for my lack of self-confidence.

This went on for the first year until I decided I was responsible for myself and my body. I went to the gym and ran with a friend. I slowly got stronger, and my long runs became my therapy. It was slow and gradual, and after a few years, I had nicer things to say to myself.

Without nourishing myself, I was miserable. Without feeding myself with kindness and grace, I was left empty. Without taking responsibility to care for myself, I was falling apart.

It doesn't take fixing anything to feed yourself with kindness. You don't have to go to the gym or lose a few pounds. A daily dose of kindness is available right now.

Have you ever seen another woman who has the thing that you are insecure about, and yet she's totally rocking it? Sitting at the pool, I saw a lady with stretch marks and extra fluff in all the same places, and she was happily wearing a bikini... **HAPPILY!** She was walking around totally rocking her awesome self. *Heck, yes!* Thank you, woman at the pool, for reminding me I don't have to wait.

Now, when I go to the pool, I am that woman. I sport my extra fluff and stretch marks with a *You're Welcome* attitude. I do it for the girl covering up in the towel. For the girl waiting to be happy when she drops those extra pounds. I do it because happiness is available right now, exactly as I am. Maybe my fluff makes me more approachable to the people that I need and need me. Maybe me having fun and being happy at the pool in this body is exactly what my kids and all those around me need. I ask myself the question that gets me past my fears and self-doubt. **HOW CAN I BE USEFUL?**

Maybe it's not the positive self-talk affirmation stuff you've heard before. But, if I say to myself, *I love my stretch marks, they are beautiful*, I don't believe that. But asking myself *how I can be useful?* That's something that I can be, despite the stretch marks. When I find a new friend at the pool because I set my fear and doubt aside and get in the water, I can feel genuinely amazed at myself. I know that I matter. I know that it has nothing to do with my stretch marks or the extra fluff. I am a person that connects with other people. I am fun. I am confident. I can make friends. All regardless of what my body looks like. That, I can believe.

Maybe you have sticky notes on your mirror right now that say lots of positive things. That's good, keep doing that. Now add **BEING**. If your sticky note says, "I love my body," but today you are not being kind to your body, change it up. Ask yourself, How can I be useful to my body today? What does my body need? What does it not need?

You can't know how much you are needed until you start showing up. You can't know how you matter in the world until you see it. When you show up, then **YOU WILL KNOW HER**. That is when you can genuinely say kind things to yourself. You will know who you are because you will see Her, and when you know Her, you will know She deserves to be nurtured and taken care of daily.

## You're Making us Look Bad

We teach our children to be nice. Our parents taught us to be nice. It's a fundamental lesson. You can hear it at the park in that mom voice, "Be Nice." And yet we are cruel to ourselves. We treat ourselves in a way that could be considered emotional abuse in a court of law. You are the one beating yourself down.

I was at the gym. One of the regular girls had recently increased her dedication. She was in the running to win the gym's summer challenge. Everyone was excited to watch her progress. She was humble, kind, and proud of herself. Her hard work made me want to work harder. Her progress gave me hope that what I was doing was effective.

A new girl joined our morning group. When she learned that Sarah was staying for a second workout, she said, "Making us all look bad, huh? Being an over achiever, are you?" The girls that heard it giggled at the sarcasm. It was playful banter, and I didn't think much of it, until we were onto our next round of exercises and Sarah picked up a challenging weight, well beyond a weight that anyone else in the group could consider. The new girl said, "Oh, now you're really making us look bad. You're really making me feel bad about myself."

No one called her out. No one defended Sarah. We all brushed it aside like it was normal. Because it is! This is normal to the point that we don't stop it, even when it's **OUT LOUD!**

When you aren't kind to yourself, it will spill out onto everyone else. Whatever you are putting into yourself is going to spill out. Maybe we all need to start consuming love and kindness for breakfast.

Pay attention to what you are feeding yourself!

## You Deserve that Win Today!

You decide to *actually* stick to your meal plan. You go to a baby shower or birthday party and of course there's cake. Your aunt offers you some cake, and you politely decline. She gives you a pouty face, making sure you know you have insulted her cake-making talent. Then your friend says, "Why aren't you eating cake? Come on, it's a special day." You stick to it, and politely and happily say, "Really, I'm okay, thank you." She rolls her eyes and replies, "Well, guess the rest of us will be pigs and eat the cake." Implying that you, not eating cake, makes everyone feel like pigs.

Why can't more people say, "Hey, good job! Yeah, if you decided to not eat cake, you should for sure follow through on that. You totally deserve that win today. Can I get you some carrots?"

That would sound more like a supportive friend helping you feel powerful.

In order for us to have that type of response to others, we have to know how to say those things to ourselves. We have to know what it feels like to stick to a personal commitment. We have to know that caring for yourself deserves someone cheering you on. If more of us were feeding ourselves with love and encouragement, we would naturally pour out love and encouragement.

*"What you put in, will spill out."*

## Feeling Awful is Not Normal

My youngest was five years old. The way I felt seemed similar to post-partum. I was tired everyday by 3 pm. My brain was foggy. My body was achy. I had no sex drive. I just felt meh.

I started going to yoga. I engaged in a food addiction recovery program. I committed to taking care of my body and my inner self.

I found answers for my back pain. I thought things would get better after that. They didn't. I felt peace and clarity from addiction recovery but the brain fog, exhaustion, and lack of sex drive were still there.

A friend recommended I get my hormones checked. So, I went to my OB-GYN. She did the blood work and told me I look normal. Maybe a little low in vitamin D, and if I wanted to do a testosterone cream she could call it in.

I tried the Vitamin D and the cream. Still nothing.

Two more years went by. Covid hit. Life got weird. I blamed my state of being on everything that was going on around me. All my friends felt the same way, so I figured this was just how 40 years of age felt.

I met a new friend who told me that she had felt the same way. She had done hormone therapy for a year and had all the symptoms go away. I thought it was too good to be true. I still thought I could fix it on my own.

Nothing was working, and I found myself in bed crying in despair for a whole weekend. It scared me. I didn't understand what was going on. Depression runs in my family, so naturally I thought... *Well, here it is. I must have depression.*

I began the search for a doctor who could help me diagnose my broken brain. Then, I remembered my friend and the hormone therapy she mentioned.

I found a similar clinic that offered the same type of therapy and called them immediately. I described all my symptoms, and for the first time, the women on the other side of the phone said, "You're not crazy, we can help you." She told me story after story of women who had felt the same way and now have relief.

The therapy wasn't in the budget. It was going to take credit cards to do it. But at this point, it was a matter of me actually living or continuing in this dark fog of existence.

At the clinic, I filled out my symptoms. I was so sad to check the depression box. *How did I get here?* The doctor noticed that I hadn't checked sleeping problems. She asked why I hadn't. I answered, "I don't have a sleeping problem. I sleep normal."

She asked, "Do you wake up in the middle of the night?" I said, "Well yeah, a few times." She questioned, "How many?" I replied, "Four to six times." She looked me straight in the eye and said, "That is not normal. You should be sleeping through the night."

"No way," I said. "I thought that wasn't a thing for adults."

Not even two days after I began the treatments, I slept through the entire night!

A week later, it was 8 p.m. and I realized I hadn't been mentally dragging myself around all day. I was still present and available. I wasn't annoyed or angry. Just a regular, generally happy human.

Three weeks in, my sex drive picked up. My body hadn't needed that for years and years. This didn't just wake me up to want sex more. This opened a door to explore all my thoughts around sex and pleasure. I found limiting beliefs about my body. I read books and watched documentaries about the female orgasm. This wasn't the horny teenager I remembered. This was a woman with a power she didn't know she had.

Only eight weeks had gone by when I shared my experience on social media. Suddenly, thousands of women were saying, "**THAT'S ME!** And my doctor said I was normal." At first, I thought... *Oh good, I'm not alone.* Over nine million views and hundreds of thousands of comments later, I realized women across the world have been living in this same fog that I had been in.

The small act of taking care of myself has now spilled over to help thousands of women know they aren't alone. They aren't crazy. They deserve to fight to feel good.

We all deserve to feel good. And when we all feel awake and alive, can you imagine what this world will be?

Visit MarcellaHill.com for more information and
providers of bioidentical hormone therapy

# Hysterectomy Party

We invite people to celebrate birthdays and baby showers. We celebrate coming of age and weddings. So many celebrations for new phases of life. I was planning to have a hysterectomy. I thought a ceremony or celebration would be appropriate. This was a new phase of my motherhood. It should be honored and celebrated.

My sister introduced me to Mother's Blessing, a beautiful alternative to a baby shower. At a baby shower, people bring gift bags filled with diapers, baby blankets, and all kinds of goodies for the new baby. Funny games are played to win party favors. Little cupcakes are served, and people make small talk and head out.

My first experience with a Mother's Blessing, I did not know the mother well, she was a friend of my sisters. They asked that everyone bring something that could be added to a bath salt mixture. I brought oatmeal. I arrived to find everyone sitting on the ground chatting. There was no baby boy banner or balloons. There were no gift bags. Just women buzzing with excitement to connect.

Then it began. We gathered in a circle and the host explained that we would introduce ourselves by announcing our matriarchal lineage while wrapping string around our wrist one at a time. Then, we were to pass the string onto the next person until the entire circle was all connected by this one strand. They started, and when it got to me, I said, "I'm Marcella, the daughter of Lisa, and the granddaughter of Linda," while wrapping the string around my wrist. Then, I passed it to the woman next to me. When the circle was complete, we cut the string and tied our new string bracelets on our wrists. We were encouraged to wear the string until the mother had her

WAKE HER UP

baby. This would allow us to be energetically connected during her journey.

Well, this was new and interesting. Not sure I was up to keeping the string on my wrist for several weeks. *Hmm...*

We started sharing what we brought for the communal bath salt mixture, and what motherhood meant to us. The communal bath salt would later be divided up into little jars and shared with everyone to take home. A woman brought lavender from her garden and told us how she'd grown it herself. She had waited for it to blossom, and she hoped that it would spark patience in the waiting. With each woman sharing, my perspective on motherhood became more and more one of pride. I didn't know any of the girls in the room except my sister. Yet, we all shared integral parts of ourselves. We shared experiences and beliefs, deep understanding and compassion.

I left that evening with my jar of bath salts created by the cumulative sharing of women. I left with the band on my wrist that reminded me each day that I am not alone and someone needed me. This experience was the most beautiful display of honoring womanhood.

Having a hysterectomy meant I was taking out a piece of my body that had allowed me the experience to birth my own children. I was moving into a new phase of womanhood. This deserved a beautiful moment. I knew I needed emotional and spiritual support. I wanted others to know they deserved it as well.

My sister hosted a Motherhood Blessing for me. A few of my closest friends were invited. The evening was filled with deep spiritual connection and an elevated understanding of who we are as women.

It was scary to share something that hadn't been done before. I was afraid that it would seem a bit pretentious to throw myself a party to honor my body. It wasn't that way at all. Sharing this transition with my friends was a beautiful experience none of us will ever forget.

Celebrating my body and honoring my experience, celebrated and honored all of the women there. They felt seen and alive.

That evening, we all woke up to a new understanding that creating was our power not our duty.

How are you nourishing yourself?

What are you feeding your mind?

What are you feeding your soul?

What are you feeding your emotions?

What are you feeding your body? What if there were no diet books, what type of eating would feel good for you?

What if there was no religion, what would bring you peace and serenity?

What if no one taught us what joy should be, how would you experience joy?

When someone tells you it's *normal* to eat the cake... pause.

When someone tells you it's *normal* to feel muted out... pause.

When everyone around you is doing it... pause.

Listen to **HER**, and then serve Her what She needs.

# WAKE HER UP

# CHAPTER 12

# GOOD MORNING!
# WE'VE BEEN EXPECTING YOU.

*I was exhausted from filling thousands of mask orders. Staying up till 3 a.m. every day for weeks to make masks and ship them out. I promised my daughter I would make banana muffins the next morning. The morning came, and I got sucked into work. There was no time for muffins. A volunteer seamstress dropped off her batch of masks. And what do you know!? Sitting right on top, homemade banana muffins.*

## A Date with a Blue Man

Things were getting out of control during the divorce. It felt like I was in a Jerry Springer show. I had to get away. I invited a friend to meet me in Las Vegas for a week. The first night, we went to see the Blue Man Group.

The show was spectacular. It felt so good to be around a million people that didn't know my depressing story. I got to be happy there. I could laugh and cheer, and no one was going to judge me for being happy while my family was falling apart.

The Blue Man Group were choosing one person from their audience of more than 1,000 people. They walked the aisles looking for a volunteer. They joked with people and kept walking around making everyone anxious. I was a few seats in from the aisle on the far side of the stage, surely our area would not be considered. A Blue Man stood at the end of our aisle, scooted down the row, past my friend and sat on my lap. Then, he took my hand and walked me up onto the stage.

This strange man taking my hand was more attention from a man than I had been shown in months, maybe years. It was more being wanted than I had felt in longer than I could remember. The Blue Man gave me flowers and sat me at a table. The scene was them acting out taking me on a date and serving me a Twinkie. Although the scene ended with disgusting goo spewing from a contraption on my chest, it was everything my soul needed to remember that I was worthy of being wanted.

There was no explaining that they would pick a girl at random out of a huge audience. The girl that was there feeling completely unwanted, disregarded, and abandoned. There I was on a stage with bright lights, an audience cheering, and part of an act that brought laughter and joy. It was so much more than a funny thing that happened.

The world was reminding me that I was worth choosing.

## Peek-a-Boo Stuff

My friend showed me a cute toy she made at a church craft night. She called it a quiet bag. It looked like a bean bag with a clear plastic window. Inside were white filler beads mixed with little trinkets. You shook it up to find the penny, barbie shoe, rubber band, and more. She was excited about it. She wanted me to help make a bunch to sell at a local Christmas boutique. So, we did.

They did well, and we made more. We kept making more and selling more. We started figuring out how to make them efficiently and cost effectively. After producing hundreds of bags, we eventually found a local manufacturer that could help us sew and assemble the bags.

I thought we could get them into toy stores and kid boutiques. I had no idea how to do that. I dressed up in business clothes and took an unfinished sample to a local toy shop. I walked in and asked who the right person was to talk to about adding a new product. For all I knew, there was one large catalog with products that all stores ordered from. I had no idea if walking in and asking was normal. I showed the woman my toy and explained what it was going to be when it was finished. She asked the cost. I didn't know and made something up. She asked what the minimum order would be. I didn't know what that meant and asked her how many she felt would be reasonable. She said a dozen. I said great, and she wrote me a check.

I kept talking to toy stores and kept getting orders.

FAO Schwarz in New York City was holding a toy audition. I mentioned it to the sewing manufacturer, and she offered to fund our trip. So, I booked the flights on her credit card, and we went to NYC. While we were there, I received an email that we had been nominated for a toy award. The toy award company just so happened to be down the street from where we were staying. We walked over and hand delivered a thank you along with their very own *Peek-a-Boo* bag. We couldn't believe that happened while we were there.

Then it was time for the audition. We had imagined what would happen if they liked it. *What if they wanted 10,000? What if they wanted more? How would we produce that many? Would we have to take it overseas? Where would we get the money?* It was exciting to be there, but we had no plan if they chose to put our toy in their stores.

Hopeful toy makers were going in and right back out. They would be in the room for less than three minutes. We were pretty discouraged as the line got shorter and shorter. I struck up a conversation with a guy who was living in Shanghai as a sourcing agent for other toy companies. He gave me his card just before we were called for our audition.

We walked into the audition room, gave our presentation, and then were asked to have a seat at the table. They were excited and discussed all the possibilities for almost 30 minutes. We walked out of that room as if we had won the lottery. We couldn't believe it. They wanted to place a large order. Now we needed to find funding and a manufacturer that could produce higher quantities for less.

As excited as we were, the next steps seemed completely impossible. We were just two moms with a fun toy idea. A few months ago, we were making them in our living room. Now we were talking about how to get to China.

We stood in line at the airport waiting to head home, still mesmerized by the experience. A guy casually asked if we were heading home or away. We shared about the toy audition and how it had gone well. I joked that we were now challenged with figuring out mass production. I will never forget the next words out of his mouth, "Well, you probably are going to need funding for that, right?"

*Are you kidding me, right now!? How is that the next thing out of his mouth? This has got to be a freaking joke!*

He said, "You should get ahold of my friend Matt when you get back." He gave us Matt's number, and I was completely skeptical. This couldn't possibly be real. The plane was delayed a few hours, and we were able to talk more in depth. It seemed that it might be legit.

I called Matt the next day. The day after that, I was in his office explaining our idea and showing him our toy. Over the next few weeks, he introduced me to angel investors and business mentors that gathered the funding needed to manufacture overseas. I called the guy who I had sat next to at FAO Schwarz. In total fear and blind faith, I wired money to China to do our first production.

We booked our first International Toy Fair in NYC for the following season. We debuted the toy and walked away with over 60 new retailers, hundreds of prospective stores, and sales reps, all willing to wait six months for our new toy.

*Peek-a-Boo Stuff* went on for four years, and was in 375 stores worldwide. The toy was featured on the Today Show as one of the top 10 travel toys of the year. We won toy awards, were featured on local news stations, and got a call from a Shark Tank producer. It was the thrill of a lifetime.

After four years, the toy industry was crumbling, and a new mandatory plastics certification was going to bankrupt us. I had to gain a license agreement quickly or we were done. I had no idea how to find a company that would take our toy. I knew a few big ones such as Mattel, Melissa & Doug, and Alex Toys, but how do you reach the person that makes this kind of decision? I did what I knew how to do and made phone calls. I started with the customer service number on their website.

Within three calls, I was in contact with the lead buyer. After speaking to a few, I reached the buyer for a large toy distributor. They had their toys in every upscale toy boutique across the nation. The buyer was immediately intrigued. He said he was going to China in two weeks and would like to source my toy while he was there. I shipped him samples. Within a month, they purchased all our current inventory, and we had a licensing agreement.

The entire experience with the toy company felt as if I was cracking a door open, and the whole world rushed in. More than I could've ever done on my own.

When you open the door, you will realize the whole world has been there waiting to cheer you on!

## Anonymous Flowers on Camera

During the Pandemic and the crazy mask making, I got a phone call from the local news station asking about our operation that we were running out of my house and off my front porch. They asked to come do a story at my house in 30 minutes. I ran to put on some mascara and a decent looking shirt. I frantically called some of my team to see if they could stop by to create a mock representation of how our operation was working. They all were available right then. The news crew showed up. We did the story, and it was so much fun.

At the very end- as if the news showing up during a pandemic wasn't already an amazing miracle-a girl pulled up right in front of my house. She got out of her car with a handful of beautiful flowers. While I was on camera, she walked up and handed me the flowers. The note was anonymous and read, "Have a great day!"

The news reporter quickly switched gears and asked how that made me feel. Immediately my whole soul was on fire. I held back tears and told the camera, "**JOY STILL EXISTS!** There is good to be found and created in the middle of a worldwide pandemic."

You can't make this stuff up! I thought I was standing on my porch explaining how to run a volunteer effort for mask making.

The world wanted to send out a reminder through me that there is still hope and joy in the midst of the scary pandemic.

# Seeker of Wool

After three years of having *Love Woolies*, I was tired and unfulfilled. I thought I would sell the company. I felt unsettled. I just had that nagging feeling that I was missing something. There was something else.

*Maybe I should I have another baby...* That was my first thought because when you are taught that your greatest joy will be to raise children, when you feel discontent, it must be that you need to have another baby. I really, really didn't want to have another child. My prayers were to ask God to help me feel excited to have another baby. I asked him for months to take away my fear.

I talked to my husband and my friends. The question seemed to roll around and around without any definitive answer. The fear of having another child wasn't going away, and the feeling of something missing was getting louder and louder.

In the middle of a prayer one night, again asking God to help me want another child, an unexpected thought entered my head. *What if I'm asking the wrong question? Have I even asked if I should have another child? What if my family is complete? What if all this discontent has nothing to do with children? Have I asked if I should sell my business? Have I even considered any other possibilities?*

So, I asked all those things not knowing what else to do. I was surprised that my prayer had ended up that way. It was as if someone had jumped in and finished it for me. I opened my eyes and looked over at my nightstand, sitting there opened were my physical scriptures.

It had been years since I opened my physical scriptures. My daughter must have been playing with them. More oddly, it was opened to a page that was entirely highlighted with red pencil. There was a note in my handwriting at the bottom of the page, "Marcella, this is who you need to be..." - 2000.

*What?! I don't have any recollection of writing this.* In 2000, I didn't have a family. I was still living in New York as a nanny.

The chapter was Proverbs 31. I had no idea what was in this chapter. I expected the scriptures to read like: Go and replenish the Earth, be meek and humble and love the Lord with all your heart, pray, and go to church, blah blah blah...

Here is what it says:

### PROVERBS 31:13

*She seeketh wool... and worketh willingly with her hands.*

*WOOL!! ARE YOU SERIOUS!?* First, how many times in the scriptures are they even talking about a woman? Secondly, where has this story about a woman seeking wool been all my life? *WHAT IS HAPPENING!?*

### PROVERBS 31:15

*She riseth also while it is yet night and giveth meat to her household and a portion to her maidens.*

As in working early and late and paying other women to help?!

### PROVERBS 31:18

*She perceiveth that her merchandise is good: her candle goeth not out by night.*

*She had MERCHANDISE!!* I had never heard about this woman in church. I was shocked!!

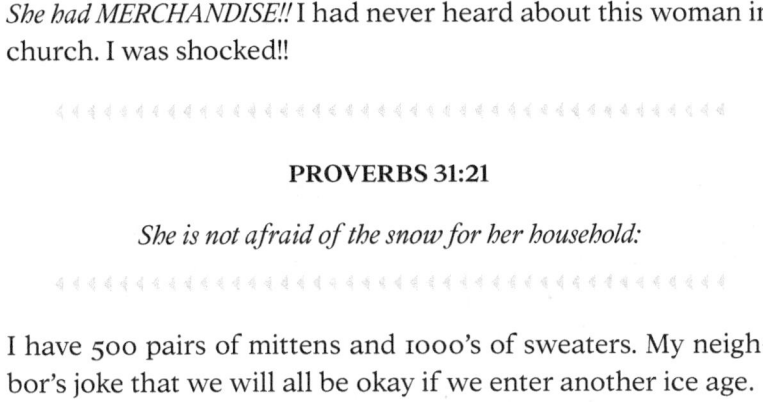

### PROVERBS 31:21

*She is not afraid of the snow for her household:*

I have 500 pairs of mittens and 1000's of sweaters. My neighbor's joke that we will all be okay if we enter another ice age.

### PROVERBS 31:24

*She maketh fine linen, and selleth it*

Selling things. There is a virtuous woman from the bible selling things! *Ummm... what do you even do with this?!*

**YOU LISTEN.**

Needless to say. I stayed in the company and kept seeking wool and making things with my hands. I thought if this was my exact right path, then there had to be millions of dollars along the way.

About a year later, a million dollars hadn't shown up, and I was feeling the stirring of something missing again. I started asking myself where I could be useful. The idea to start sharing some of my personal stories on social media came to the front of my mind.

That didn't make sense. My stories weren't going to help sell mittens, but I wasn't going to argue. I started sharing my experiences and what I had learned from them. My soul lit up. I started to connect with women hearing my stories.

*Maybe I was being called to be a motivational speaker... But how would I run Love Woolies and do public speaking?* They didn't go together at all!

I was asked to do a scrunchie making tutorial for a young women's youth group along with sharing an uplifting message. I showed a sweater that had holes in it and told a few stories about times in my life that I had felt ruined. Experiences that left me knowing I would never be the same. Situations that made me feel like I was useless.

I started cutting the holes out of the sweater. I told more stories of times I was able to look past the fear and past the destruction. I held up the good pieces and let the other parts go. More stories of getting creative with my life and how it had resulted in something beyond my imagination. Just like the messed-up sweater becoming beautiful, luxurious scrunchies. It was a fun little lesson for about eight girls and four adult leaders in a living room.

A woman asked if I did public speaking. I told her it was odd that she would ask me that because I had felt that I needed to start. She said that her family owned Pinners Conference, and this was exactly the type of thing they were looking for.

All at once, my company of repurposing wool sweaters encompassed all of my life lessons. It held what I had a desire to share and teach. I had been standing in it this entire time and had never seen the message of *Creating Joy from the Flaws*.

A few months and miracles later, I was in Minneapolis speaking to a room of women, sharing the sweater message. I watched souls wake up and hear things they had never considered. I stood in a space that clearly was well beyond anything I could've ever imagined or created.

I had opened the door, and the world was waiting.

My company is now centered around this message of *Creating Joy from the Flaws*. It is my heart and soul. We no longer sell stuff. We sell **JOY** that inspires you to look past the flaws in your life.

## *Ready Go*

She sat on the edge of the mountain paralyzed in fear. We were repelling for the first time. Some of the girls had done this before. We watched a few girls go down the steep cliff. They had made it down safely without any trouble. It still looked terrifying. I watched as the girl that seemed the most fearful got hooked in. The guide told her to lay back. He told her to pause and breathe. He had her look around and take in the view from the top. He calmly and confidently showed her how to use her hands with her rope to break and to go. He took off the safety and told her she was ready to go. She shook her head, no. He said, "Yes, just lean back and do what I've explained. You've got this."

She leaned back in total fear but also trust. She allowed the rope to slowly move through her hands as she started to descend the side of the mountain. He guided her steps, reminding her to lean back and let the rope do the work. Each step was less scary. As soon as she could see that she was going to make it, she laughed. Her feet touched the ground, she smiled, and was amazed at what she had done.

Then, it was my turn. Watching her do it didn't make it less scary, but it did make me think if she can do it, then I can do it. I walked to the edge of the mountain, he talked me through all the same steps. He told me to let go with one hand and wave at the camera. I still didn't trust it. I was hanging off the side of a mountain! *I could die!* But I took a deep breath and let go. I nervously waved at the camera.

He told me to look around and enjoy seeing things that not many would see that day. I couldn't enjoy it much, I was too scared, but looked around anyway. I went very slowly, trying to learn how it works. Trying to understand how tight to hold on and when to let go.

I made it. I didn't die. Then I went again. It was still scary to go over that initial edge, but during that second repel, I dared to jump and hang upside down!

I used to think that we were given mountains to climb because we needed to become stronger and pick up missing pieces of ourselves along the journey. I believed trials happened to grow a characteristic that we were missing. I don't believe that anymore.

I believe that we have all the tools and all the characteristics we need to show the world how it looks to climb the mountains we are given. We were born with all the tools. You might have to learn how to use them, but you have everything you need for everything you will ever face in this life. It's already in you.

You just have to wake up, throw the covers off, put your pants on, eat some breakfast, and open the door!

Your way of doing this life, your way of using your tools, your stories, your setbacks, they are the guide for everyone around you. They are the motivation, the lessons, and the hope.

**YOU**... You are the thing that makes it possible for others to travel their journey.

We need **YOU**. We need you to **WAKE UP!** We need you to find out who you are and **BE HER.**

Your alarm is going off, the sun is coming up, it is a new day, it's time to go,

# *Wake* HER UP.

It's your turn to Wake HER Up.

I hope you will join the awakening at **MarcellaHill.com**

# WAKE HER UP SUMMARY

*Cause sometimes you don't have time to sleep in
and slowly roll out of bed.*

*You got to wake up, throw your hair up in a scrunchie, put
your pants on, and run out the door.*

## 1 - Living Asleep

*If you never wake up, are you really alive?*

## 2 - No More Blanky

*What would you be without the thought?*
*—Byron Katie*

## 3 - Open Your Eyes

*If you never see what's going on, you risk living.*

## 4- Kick Them Out

*Mean people don't belong in your bed or your head.*

## 5 - Its Not Working, Going Back to Bed

*Trying Counts*

## 6 - Rip Off the Covers

*The world is no longer happening to you.*

*You were meant to happen to the world.*

## 7 - Get Out of Bed

*No one is coming.*

## 8 - Turn On The Light

*Your joy is your air. Without it, you aren't living.*

## 9 - Brush Your Teeth

*Be still. You will be found.*

## 10 - Put Your Pants On

*It's not about having the right pants.*

*It's how you show up in the pants you have.*

## 11 - Don't Skip Breakfast

*What you put in, will spill out.*

## 12 - Good Morning! We've Been Expecting You

*If you think something's missing ... It's probably* **YOU.**

# WAKE HER UP

# ACKNOWLEDGMENTS:

Thank you to my dear husband, Tage, for allowing me to be all of me. Your ability to love me when I'm awful and when I'm succeeding is a gift. I adore sharing this experience of life with you. Through this process of finding myself, I have fallen madly in love with you. Thank you for being here for all of my journey. Thank you for waking me up to the understanding that I am worth keeping and loving with all my good,my bad, and with all my crazy dreams and failures. At the end of the day, it's you I want to have hold me. It's you that I look for in the crowd. It's you that I know will catch me when I fall, and who will cheer when I rise. Because of you, my eyes have been opened to what love is. I love you.

Shellie, you were there during my darkest moments. You answered every call. You carried me with your voice through the horror of losing a life I loved. It is your passion and love for writing that made me think this was possible. Your talent and joy awakened a joy within me, I didn't know was there. Thank you for you.

Thank you to my Mom, for encouraging me and supporting me from the moment you knew I existed. Thank you for saying yes to all my crazy ideas. All the lemonade stands, the Halloween costumes, the time at dance concerts, the meals, the money, the enduring boyfriends, all of it. Thank you for believing in me.

Thank you to my Dad, for showing me how to take ideas and make them reality. For your sound reasoning and courage to say hard things. Thank you for your passion and interests that have lit up my life. It's a thrill to watch you live.

Thank you to my children for your independence. For getting yourself a bowl of cereal when Mom is pursuing her dreams.

Thank you for leaning into your talents and passions. You have reminded me what joy is, what it looks like, and how to find it. Never put your dreams aside. Everyone around you needs them.

Thank you to my siblings, for your love, encouragement, and support. You're all younger and wiser. I am encouraged by each of your lives.

Thank you to my in-laws, you have welcomed me and my children into your life with open arms. Your unconditional love and acceptance have provided a soft place to land. Your courage to dream and live a life you design has been awakening for me and your son.

Thank you to my friends who have endured my endless dreaming and learning. Thank you for all the time you have spent listening and cheering. Thank you for your patience and unconditional support. Thank you for going through this life with me. Thank you for praying with me, crying with me, celebrating with me. This world is brighter with you showing up. Let's keep lighting it up!

Thank you to the Love Woolies team for being a part of building my dream. Thank you for enduring my crazy ideas and compulsive nature. You have listened, encouraged, celebrated, and cried through my entrepreneurial journey. Thank you.

Thank you to my customers who have opened their hearts to our message. Thank you for your support and belief in what we do at Love Woolies. Thank you for showing up with all your love and encouragement. I found the message of Joy from the flaws because of you. Thank you.

Thank you to Tiffany who dropped into my life with the talent and ability to organize my stories. Thank you for knowing how to pull my voice out onto the pages. Thank you for the stillness you created to find the title. The world needs you, there are so many stories to tell, and you have the power to put them on paper.

Thank you to Lil and your talent to help me make this a reality. Thank you for your belief in my words. Thank you for your knowledge and ability to bring this to the women who need it.

Thank you to my Creators for this beautiful world I have the privilege of experiencing. Thank you for the people in it that light up my soul and expand my understanding. Thank you for showing me unconditional love and happiness. Thank you for building joy and passion inside my soul.

Thank you for all of you. I started this book for myself. And now that it's here, it doesn't feel like mine anymore. I still have much more awakening to do. I am so grateful I get to do it with you. Thank you for listening to your inner knowing. Thank you for giving my words a chance to wake up your soul. Thank you for sharing in this existence with me. Thank you for **YOU**.

# *Wake* HER UP.

I'm thrilled to present my stories to the world in hopes it will awaken other women to find their true selves. I look forward to sharing our journey of insights, stumbles, trials, and triumphs with each other.

Let's wake up and LIVE together!

*"We were meant to happen to the world, not the other way around."*

— MARCELLA HILL

*Marcella Hill*

Hi! I'm Marcella Hill, this pretty much sums me up:

- Loud talker on the phone and on stage
- Use to be Mormon
- Food addict in recovery (depending on the day)
- Fearless, except if whales come to mind
- Divorced and remarried
- Mother to four kiddos who reside in three different homes
- A business owner who has had both failures and successes
- Surviving and thriving with teenagers
- Sober with an occasional glass of wine
- Organizer for books, salads, walking, and kids
- Believer that everything is for our good, except mosquitoes

# WAKE HER UP

*Acknowledgments:*

# WAKE HER UP